THE MOST FANTASTIC ATLAS OF THE WHOLE WIDE WORLD

by the Brainwaves

Illustrated by Lisa Swerling and Ralph Lazar

written by Simon Adams

CONTENTS

8–9	WORLD WE LIVE ON
10 & 15	NORTH AMERICA
11–14	CRAZY GOLF
16–17	WORLD'S STRUCTURE
18 & 23	SOUTH AMERICA
19–22	CARNIVAL PARADE
24–25	WORLD'S SURFACE
26 & 31	AFRICA
27–30	AN AFRICAN ABODE
32–33	WEATHER AND CLIMATE
34 & 39	EUROPE
35–38	EUROVISION ART SHOW
40–41	OCEANS
42 & 47	ASIA
43–46	BIZARRE BAZAAR
48–49	WORLD'S PEOPLE
50 & 55	OCEANIA
51–54	BEACH BARBECUE
56–57	POLAR REGIONS
58	COMPARATIVELY SPEAKING
59–61	Glossary and Index

DK

LONDON, NEW YORK, MELBOURNE,
MUNICH, and DELHI

Project Editor Niki Foreman
Designer Jim Green

Managing Editor Linda Esposito
Managing Art Editor Diane Thistlethwaite

U.S. Editor John Searcy

Consultant Dr. Michael K. Goodman
Senior Cartographic Editor Simon Mumford

Jacket Editor Mariza O'Keeffe
Indexer Lynn Bresler

Publishing Manager Andrew Macintyre
Category Publisher Laura Buller

Production Controller Angela Graef

First published in the United States in 2008
by DK Publishing
375 Hudson Street, New York, New York 10014

Copyright © 2008 Dorling Kindersley Limited
A Penguin Company

08 09 10 11 12 10 9 8 7 6 5 4 3 2 1
BD611 - 07/08

A catalog record for this book is available from
the Library of Congress.

ISBN: 978-0-7566-4009-5

Color reproduction by
Media Development & Printing Ltd, Bath

Printed and bound by Hung Hing, Hong Kong

Discover more at
www.dk.com
www.thebrainwaves.com

This way

That way

It's the
Brainwaves on tour!

Wait for me!

Cat's out of the bag...

About this book

Featuring the Brainwaves—those little people with big ideas—this fascinating atlas takes us on a tantalizing tour of the world as it's never been seen before. A key feature is the six double gatefolds, each of which focuses on one of six continents: North America, South America, Africa, Europe, Asia, and Oceania. In addition there are special features on a comprehensive range of subjects, including Earth's structure, the world's people, oceans, and weather and climate.

Introduction provides an overview of the continent.

Wacky illustrated maps reveal the physical attributes of each continent.

Pull-out features provide information about important details.

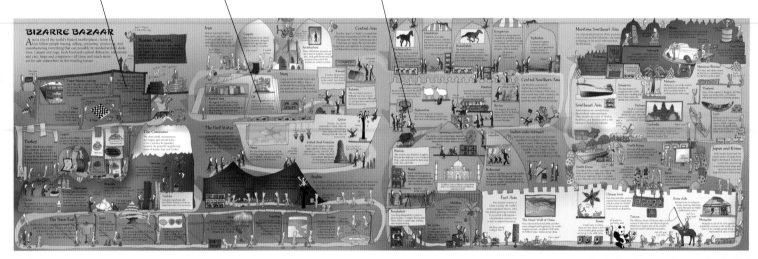

Introduction

The top two pages of each gatefold is where we begin our journey, with highly imaginative, illustrated maps portraying the physical features of each continent.

Every country on the continent is represented in an imaginative way

Captions divulge fascinating facts about each country.

Follow the Brainwaves as they tour each landscape.

Folded-out gatefold

The gatefold folds out to reveal a landscape bursting with information about the people, customs, industries, and famous landmarks of each country on the continent.

The Brainwaves have a lot to say!

Annotated diagrams explain the geographical features and processes at work on Earth.

Special features

In between each of the gatefolds, we take a look at the geography of our world, from the underwater landscape of the deep seas to each region's weather and climate, and from the rocks and processes that have shaped our world to the diversity of its people.

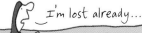
I'm lost already...

Look out for me!

Throughout the book, I'll be busy loading up my backpack with trinkets and filling my brain with scintillating information to create a special surprise at the end of the book.

WORLD WE LIVE ON

Our home, Planet Earth, is one of eight planets that orbit the Sun—a vast, hot star that gives out light and heat and supports life on Earth. The Sun is just one of about 200 billion stars in a galaxy called the Milky Way, itself one of about 100 billion galaxies that make up the Universe. Many of these stars have planets that orbit around them, but, as far as we know, Earth is the only planet that supports life.

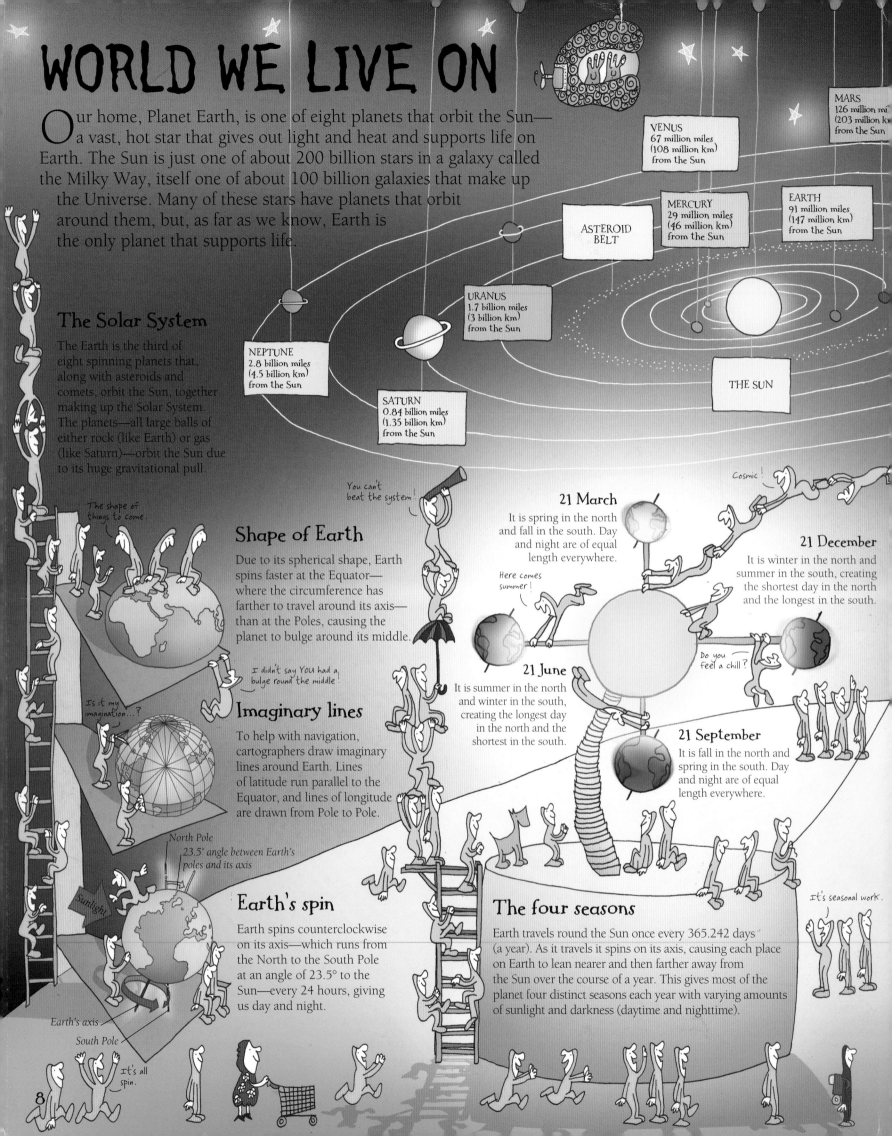

MARS
126 million mi
(203 million km)
from the Sun

VENUS
67 million miles
(108 million km)
from the Sun

MERCURY
29 million miles
(46 million km)
from the Sun

EARTH
91 million miles
(147 million km)
from the Sun

ASTEROID BELT

URANUS
1.7 billion miles
(3 billion km)
from the Sun

NEPTUNE
2.8 billion miles
(4.5 billion km)
from the Sun

SATURN
0.84 billion miles
(1.35 billion km)
from the Sun

THE SUN

The Solar System

The Earth is the third of eight spinning planets that, along with asteroids and comets, orbit the Sun, together making up the Solar System. The planets—all large balls of either rock (like Earth) or gas (like Saturn)—orbit the Sun due to its huge gravitational pull.

Shape of Earth

Due to its spherical shape, Earth spins faster at the Equator—where the circumference has farther to travel around its axis—than at the Poles, causing the planet to bulge around its middle.

The shape of things to come.

I didn't say you had a bulge round the middle!

Imaginary lines

To help with navigation, cartographers draw imaginary lines around Earth. Lines of latitude run parallel to the Equator, and lines of longitude are drawn from Pole to Pole.

Is it my imagination...?

North Pole
23.5° angle between Earth's poles and its axis

Sunlight

Earth's axis
South Pole

It's all spin.

Earth's spin

Earth spins counterclockwise on its axis—which runs from the North to the South Pole at an angle of 23.5° to the Sun—every 24 hours, giving us day and night.

You can't beat the system!

Cosmic!

21 March
It is spring in the north and fall in the south. Day and night are of equal length everywhere.

Here comes summer!

21 December
It is winter in the north and summer in the south, creating the shortest day in the north and the longest in the south.

21 June
It is summer in the north and winter in the south, creating the longest day in the north and the shortest in the south.

Do you feel a chill?

21 September
It is fall in the north and spring in the south. Day and night are of equal length everywhere.

It's seasonal work.

The four seasons

Earth travels round the Sun once every 365.242 days (a year). As it travels it spins on its axis, causing each place on Earth to lean nearer and then farther away from the Sun over the course of a year. This gives most of the planet four distinct seasons each year with varying amounts of sunlight and darkness (daytime and nighttime).

NORTH AMERICA

The continent of North America is home to more than 500 million people, most of whom speak English or Spanish. In its north is Canada, a beautiful country with the largest group of French speakers outside France, and to its south is the United States and Caribbean Islands, the former being the richest and most powerful country in the world, while the latter attracts thousands of tourists to its beautiful beaches.

No roads

Without any roads, Greenland's people get around by plane and helicopter.

...processing, especially of shrimp, is the main industry in Greenland.

We in igloos—houses built of snow blocks frozen together by ice.

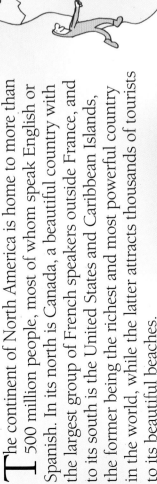

Greenland

Greenland is the world's largest island, of which four-fifths is covered by a thick ice cap. It is home to about 57,000 people and is part of Denmark.

Canada

A country rich in natural resources and beautiful scenery, Canada is the world's second largest country but also one of the emptiest, with a population of just 32 million who mainly live in cities close to its southern border.

Prairies

The farms on the Prairies of southern Alberta, Saskatchewan, and Manitoba are among the largest in the world.

Maple

The maple leaf is the national symbol of Canada and appears in the middle of the flag.

Nunavut

In 1999 a homeland called Nunavut was set up for the 30,000 Inuit in the north of Canada.

Totem poles

Some of the First Nation peoples erected wooden totem poles to record their families' histories.

Tar sands

The world's second largest reserves of oil, after Saudi Arabia, lie in Alberta in the form of tar sands—a mixture of crude oil, sand, and water.

Ore mining

Canada has vast reserves of important minerals such as potash, uranium, and asbestos.

Calgary Stampede

The world-famous rodeo at the annual Calgary Stampede tests cowboys' and cowgirls' skills.

Lacrosse

The rules of lacrosse were recorded by Canadian William George Beers in 1867, and the game has remained popular in Canada ever since.

Hockey

The national winter sport of Canada, hockey is hugely popular and played throughout the country.

Niagara Falls

The colossal Niagara Falls sits on the border between the U.S. and Canada.

Cod fishing

The Grand Banks off the southeast coast of Newfoundland were the richest cod fisheries in the world, but overfishing has drastically reduced stocks.

The Rocky Mountains

The Rockies run down the west of Canada, separating the Prairies from the Pacific coastline.

CN Tower

At a dizzying 1,465ft (447m) high, the world's highest public observation deck is boasted by the CN Tower.

Québec

Once ruled by France, the vast majority of Québec's people still speak French as their main language.

United States of America

Stretching across the North American continent from the Atlantic to the Pacific coast, the United States is made up of 50 very different states and is home to 300 million people.

The Aleuts

In western Alaska and the Aleutian Islands are the Aleuts, who live off the sea and are skilled hunters.

Walt Disney World

Walt Disney's cartoon creations can all be found at the theme park Walt Disney World in Orlando, Florida.

Surfin' USA

The huge Pacific rollers that crash onto the west coast make the California beaches an ideal place to surf.

Statue of Liberty

The 305ft- (93m-) tall Statue of Liberty stands in New York Harbor, a gift to the American people from the French in 1886.

White House

The White House in Washington is the home of the U.S. president, who runs the country from the famous Oval Office.

Tickertape parade

American heroes parade through New York to streams of tickertape floating down on them from the skyscrapers above.

Yellowstone

The oldest and largest national park in the United States, Yellowstone contains more than half the world's geysers.

Tornadoes

Several hundred twisters a year run through "Tornado Alley" in Oklahoma, Kansas, and Missouri.

Hollywood

The center of the U.S. film industry, Hollywood, California, is home to the annual star-studded Oscar awards.

HOLLYWOOD

Cowboys

Cowboys look after the vast herds of cattle that roam America's Wild West, although today most ride in 4x4 pickups.

Baseball

Baseball is the national game of the United States. The winning teams of the National League and the American League compete each year in the World Series.

Jazz

One of America's greatest contributions to modern music, jazz originated in New Orleans around 1900.

Mississippi

Huge paddle-steamers sail up and down the Mississippi River, traditionally carrying people and freight, but today carrying mainly tourists.

Gulf of Mexico

The Gulf of Mexico is rich in oil, although massive hurricanes often stop production during the fall.

Computers

The U.S. computer industry is based on the west coast, employing hundreds of thousands of people developing new software.

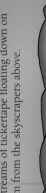
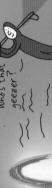

Pluto

Discovered in 1930, Pluto was initially categorized as the ninth planet in the Solar System. But its small size and irregular orbit round the Sun caused many astronomers to doubt its status as a planet, and it was reclassified in 2006 as minor planet 134340.

JUPITER
460 million miles
(741 million km)
from the Sun

The Moon

The closest object to us in space is our moon—a large rocky ball with a diameter one-quarter that of Earth. The Moon orbits Earth every 29.53 days—a lunar month. It has no light of its own but "shines" by reflecting the Sun's light.

Eclipses

Occasionally the Moon's orbit takes it directly between the Sun and Earth, preventing the Sun's light from reaching Earth. This is a solar eclipse. A lunar eclipse occurs when the Moon passes into Earth's shadow.

TOTAL SOLAR ECLIPSE

Sunlight — Moon — Moon's inner shadow
Moon's outer shadow — Earth

Sunlight — Earth's inner shadow
Earth — Moon
Earth's outer shadow — LUNAR ECLIPSE

EXOSPHERE
430–500 miles (700–800km)

THERMOSPHERE
50–430 miles (80–700km)

Communications satellite

High-level aurora or colored lights

Space shuttle

Space station

Low-level aurora

IONOSPHERE (WITHIN THE THERMOSPHERE)
62–190 miles (100–300km)

MESOSPHERE
30–50 miles (50–80km)

Weather balloon

Radio signals are bounced around the world off the ionosphere

STRATOSPHERE
7–30 miles (12–50km)

Passenger airplane

TROPOSPHERE
0–7 miles (0–12km)

Helicopter

Sky divers

Earth's atmosphere

Held in place by gravity, the atmosphere is a layer of water vapor, fine dust, and gases, including nitrogen and oxygen, that encases Earth. The atmosphere extends for about 500 miles (800km) until it simply fades into space.

NORTH AMERICA

The world's third largest continent after Asia and Africa, North America contains the ice-covered island of Greenland to the north and the tropical Caribbean Islands to the south, as well as the mainland of North and Central America. The continent's wide-ranging landscape varies from frozen tundra in the north, through high mountain chains and flat, fertile plains, to hot, dry deserts, and lush rain forest in the south.

The Great Lakes

A series of five freshwater lakes that form the natural boundary between the U.S. and Canada, the Great Lakes are the largest body of fresh water in the world and include the immense Niagara Falls. The lakes are drained by the St. Lawrence River, which flows northeast into the Atlantic Ocean.

The Great Plains

Between the Rocky Mountains to the west and the Missouri and Mississippi rivers to the east, lie the Great Plains or Prairies—the breadbasket of the continent. Crops including wheat, flax, and cotton are grown here, and the area supports vast herds of cattle and flocks of sheep.

The Rockies

The Rocky Mountains stretch down the west coast of North America from Alaska in the north to New Mexico in the south. The snow-capped mountains are popular with skiers and mountaineers and home to an array of wildlife, including elk, moose, and grizzly bears.

Km
Miles
100 200 300 400 500 600

Nuuk, GREENLAND (to Denmark)

DAVIS ST

BAFFIN BAY

ARCTIC OCEAN

BEAUFORT SEA

Alaska (to USA)

BERING SEA

WORLD'S STRUCTURE

Our Earth is a complex ball of different chemical elements combined together to form rocks and minerals that are constantly on the move. The tectonic plates that, pieced together, make up Earth's shell are constantly shifting and breaking up the landscape. As continents drift and jostle across Earth's surface, massive mountain ranges are thrown up, volcanoes erupt, and earthquakes shake the ground beneath our feet.

Crust—Earth's thin, outer layer

Earth's layers

Earth is made up of different layers, with a solid metal inner core, made hard by immense pressure, and an outer core of molten metals. Wrapped around the core is a layer of solid rock, which turns molten as it edges toward Earth's crust—the rigid layer of Earth's shell.

Hmm, the thermometer's melted!

Inside Earth

Dig just below the surface of the Earth and the temperature drops slightly. However, from there on down the temperature rises to be fantastically hot, so that by the time you reach Earth's inner core, the temperature has soared to a scorching 6,700°F (3,700°C).

Aaargh!

I'm shaken to the core.

He's in his element.

Mantle—soild rock, with liquid magma in the upper mantle

Outer core—liquid metals

Inner core—solid metals

Stop making things up.

Woof!

Oxygen 28%

Other elements 0.6%

Iron 35%

Nickel 2.7%

Magnesium 17%

Sulphur 2.7%

Silicon 13%

Calcium 0.6%

Aluminium 0.4%

Chemical makeup

More than 80 separate elements make up Earth. The largest component is iron, which is thought to be found largely in the core. Oxygen, magnesium, and silicon are also important elements in Earth's structure, and occur in large quantities.

I've got a lot on my plate.

Magnetic North Pole

I feel a strange attraction.

Geographic North Pole

Magnetic Earth

The dense core of iron that makes up Earth's core turns it into a giant magnet which, like all magnets, has a north and south pole. These two magnetic poles are different from the geographical poles, and move around as much as 25 miles (40km) a year as Earth's magnetic field varies.

Magnetic South Pole

Geographic South Pole

200 million years ago

180 million years ago

65 million years ago

Get a move on.

On the move

The world's continents sit on top of moving tectonic plates that float on Earth's upper mantle. These plates were once joined together, but gradually broke up and drifted apart to form the continents we know today.

Mexico

With more than 107 million people, Mexico is the largest Spanish-speaking country in the world and was once the center of the mighty Aztec Empire.

Mexico City

The mountains that surround Mexico City trap air pollution, causing a thick layer of smog to blanket the city.

Has anyone seen a city?

Let's get spicy

Mexican food

Burritos, guacamole, and chilies are just some of Mexico's world-famous foods.

Day of the Dead

Mexicans celebrate the Day of the Dead each year, when the souls of the dead are said to visit their loved ones.

Mexican Wave

The ripple effect of the Mexican Wave is famous and so-named after spectators "waved" at the 1986 World Cup in Mexico.

Wave!

Hello!

¡Hola!

Mariachi bands

Traditional folk musicians wearing national costume are popular performers throughout Mexico.

Caballeros

Mexican cowboys, known as caballeros locally, are skilled horse riders.

I'm feeling hoarse.

Yucatan

The limestone of the Yucatan peninsula has worn away in some places to form spectacular cenotes (sink holes) and caves.

Guatemala

The largest and most populated of the seven Central American states, Guatemala is mountainous with a fertile plain along the Pacific coast. More than half its people are Amerindians—descendants of the original Maya inhabitants.

This is ruining my game.

Tikal Temple

The Maya built huge pyramid-shaped temples, many of which were only recently rediscovered and restored.

Belize

Once a British colony, Belize is the only English-speaking country in Central America. It is the least populated country in the region and half its land is heavily forested.

The world's your lobster.

Aaargh!

Barrier reef

Belize's barrier reef is the second largest in the world, and protects the country's low-lying, swampy coastal plain.

This place is bananas.

Honduras

Mountainous Honduras has a long coastline on the Caribbean Sea and a short, sheltered outlet to the Pacific. Almost all of its 7.2 million people are Mestizos—mixed Spanish-Amerindian.

Bananas

Here, as elsewhere in the region, the main crop is bananas, although coffee, fruit, and flowers are also grown for export.

Help!

Hurricane Mitch

In 1998 Honduras and neighboring Nicaragua suffered huge devastation by Hurricane Mitch.

El Salvador

The smallest and most densely populated of the Central American republics, El Salvador lies on the Pacific coast and grows coffee and other crops for export.

Sisal

Sisal plants are grown to yield a stiff fibre that is used to make strong rope and bags for such exports as coffee and cereal.

It's in the bag.

Volcanoes

A line of 20 volcanoes runs through the country, providing cheap and plentiful geothermal energy.

Explosive stuff!

Nicaragua

The fertile volcanic soil along the Pacific coastline forms the main farming region in Nicaragua. Corn, beans, and sorghum are harvested twice a year while coffee, cotton, and bananas are grown for export.

Lake Nicaragua

Dominating the south of Nicaragua, Lake Nicaragua is the only freshwater lake in the world to contain sea fish, including scary sharks and vigorous swordfish.

Shark!

Costa Rica

One of the richest countries in the region, Costa Rica was the first country in the region to grow coffee, which today is one of its main exports, as well as bananas.

Cream and sugar, please.

Ecotourism

Costa Rica's forests and wildlife are today protected in reserves and national parks, which attract ecotourists from around the world.

Where's that chameleon?

Aluminum

Costa Rica has large reserves of bauxite that are smelted to make aluminum.

That smells my heart.

Panama

Long, thin Panama is the most southerly country in Central America, forming a land link to South America. Its climate is hot and humid with heavy rainfall, enabling a wide range of crops to be grown in its fertile soil.

Panama Canal

The Panama Canal is an important sea route between the Atlantic and Pacific oceans.

Hey!

Shared island

The island of Hispaniola is shared by two nations—Haiti (the first independent nation in the Caribbean) in the west and the Dominican Republic in the east.

I can't see the forest for the trees.

Missed!

Tree loss

Both nations suffer from deforestation, as trees are cut down for firewood or to clear the ground for agriculture.

Woo!

Windward Islands

The seven island groups of the Windwards are mainly hilly and very fertile, with Grenada being one of the major spice-producing nations in the world.

FINISH

I've got a pounding headache.

Steel-pan drums

Providing music for Trinidad's annual carnival, the steel-pan drums were invented on the island.

Cricket

The British introduced cricket to the West Indies, where it is now a major sport.

Music

The slums of Kingston, the island's capital, have produced music styles such as ska, reggae, and ragga (dancehall).

Rastafarians

The Rastafarian religion began in Jamaica in the 1930s. Rastafarians believe that God will lead black people home to the promised land of Ethiopia.

Irie, mon.

Jamaica

The English-speaking island of Jamaica is rich in minerals—it is the world's fourth largest producer of bauxite—and has a fertile landscape with beautiful beaches.

Tourism

With its fine beaches and cheap hotels, the Dominican Republic is the Caribbean's most popular tourist destination.

Fore!

Montserrat

The Soufrière Hills volcano exploded on Montserrat in 1997, making two-thirds of the island uninhabitable.

Who's paying?

Let's go Dutch.

St. Martin

Split between French and Dutch rule, St. Martin's people speak two languages and use two currencies.

Leeward Islands

A mixture of independent nations and British, French, Dutch, and U.S. colonies, the Leeward Islands are so-called because they are in the "lee" of the Windward Islands that shelter them from the prevailing winds.

Cuba

The largest island in the Caribbean Sea, Cuba is made up of mountains, rolling hills, and flat plains. It is very fertile and rich in nickel, cobalt, and other minerals.

Cigars

Cuba's warm days and cool nights are ideal for growing tobacco, which is cut, dried, and rolled to make the world-famous Cuban cigars.

Is it a Cuban cube?

Would you like sugar?

Sugar cane

Sugar and its many by-products account for half of Cuba's total exports, along with coffee, tobacco, fish, and minerals.

Puerto Rico

Spanish-speaking Puerto Rico has been a U.S. territory since 1898, and many U.S. companies produce cheap goods here to sell back home.

Population

Puerto Rico has one of the highest population densities in the world, with 3.8 million people living tightly packed on the island.

Stop crowding me!

Bahamas

The island chain of the Bahamas lies northeast of Cuba in the Atlantic Ocean, and is a wealthy financial center. Only 30 of the 700 islands are inhabited.

Tourism

More than 40 percent of the Bahamas' population works in the tourist industry, mainly servicing the many cruise liners that visit the islands.

I'm cruisin' through life

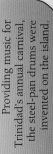

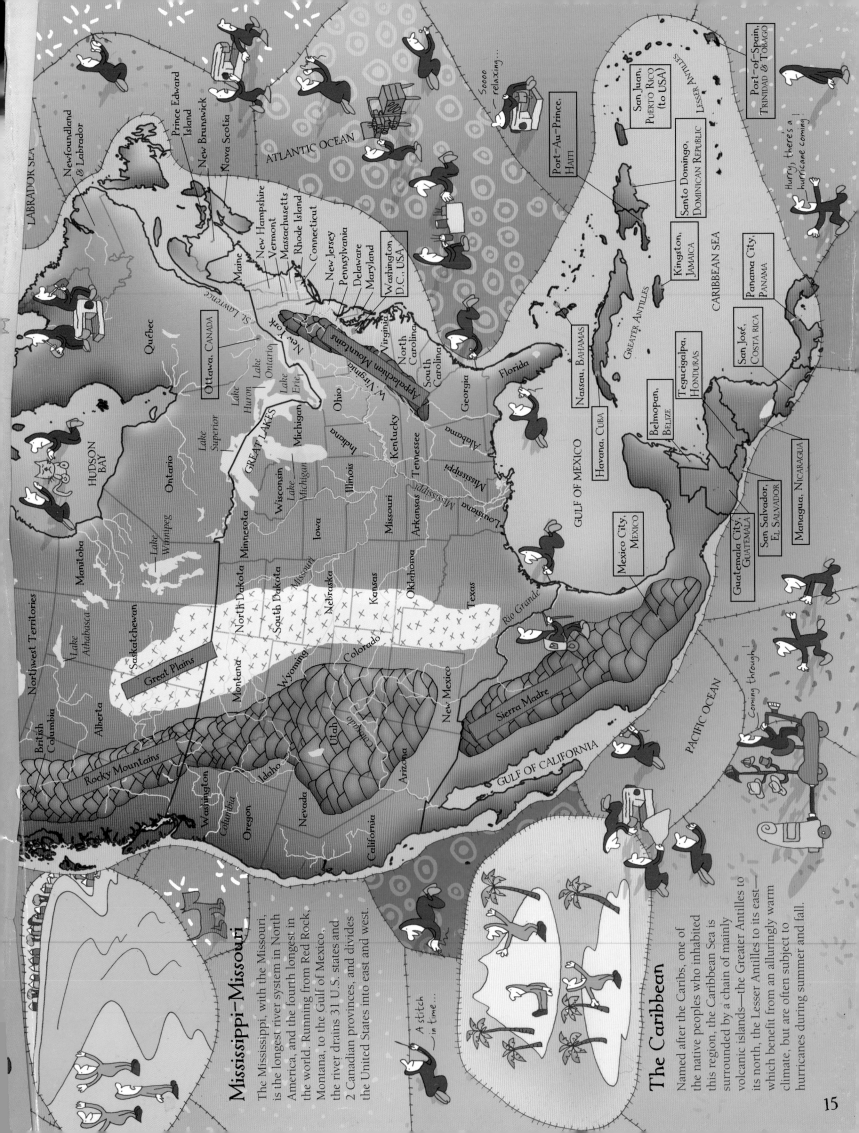

Mississippi–Missouri

The Mississippi, with the Missouri, is the longest river system in North America, and the fourth longest in the world. Running from Red Rock, Montana, to the Gulf of Mexico, the river drains 31 U.S. states and 2 Canadian provinces, and divides the United States into east and west.

The Caribbean

Named after the Caribs, one of the native peoples who inhabited this region, the Caribbean Sea is surrounded by a chain of mainly volcanic islands—the Greater Antilles to its north, the Lesser Antilles to its east—which benefit from an alluringly warm climate, but are often subject to hurricanes during summer and fall.

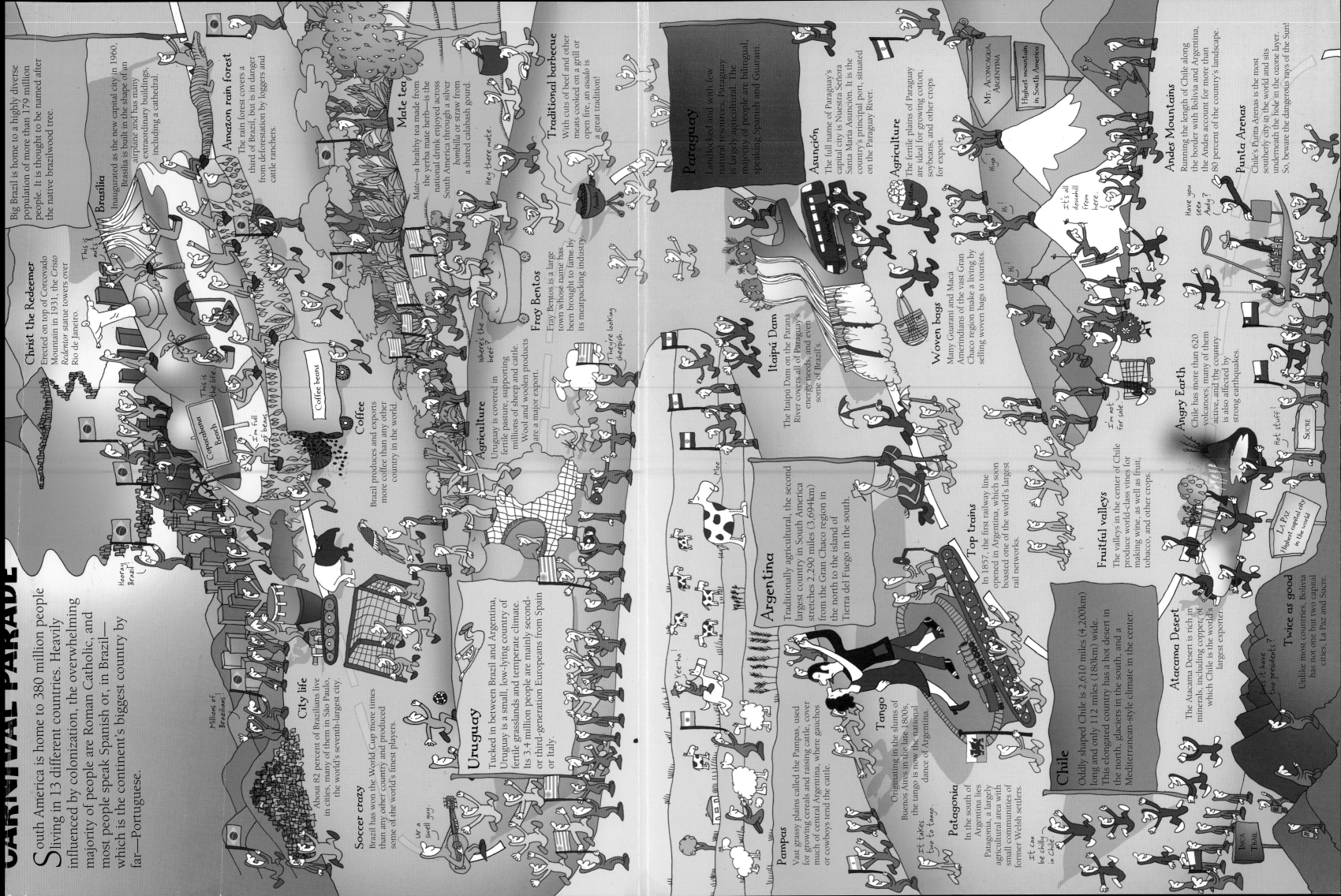

CARNIVAL PARADE

South America is home to 380 million people living in 13 different countries. Heavily influenced by colonization, the overwhelming majority of people are Roman Catholic, and most people speak Spanish or, in Brazil—which is the continent's biggest country by far—Portuguese.

Christ the Redeemer
Erected on top of Corcovado Mountain in 1931, the *Cristo Redentor* statue towers over Rio de Janeiro.

Brasília
Big Brazil is home to a highly diverse population of more than 179 million people. It is thought to be named after the native brazilwood tree.

Inaugurated as the new capital city in 1960, Brasília is built in the shape of an airplane and has many extraordinary buildings, including a cathedral.

Amazon rain forest
The rain forest covers a third of Brazil, but is in danger from deforestation by loggers and cattle ranchers.

Mate tea
Mate—a healthy tea made from the yerba mate herb—is the national drink enjoyed across South America through a silver *bombilla* or straw from a shared calabash gourd.

Traditional barbecue
With cuts of beef and other meats cooked on a grill or open fire, an *asado* is a great tradition!

Coffee
Brazil produces and exports more coffee than any other country in the world.

City life
About 82 percent of Brazilians live in cities, many of them in São Paulo, the world's seventh-largest city.

Soccer crazy
Brazil has won the World Cup more times than any other country and produced some of the world's finest players.

Uruguay
Tucked in between Brazil and Argentina, Uruguay is a small, low-lying country of fertile grasslands and temperate climate. Its 3.4 million people are mainly second- or third-generation Europeans from Spain or Italy.

Agriculture
Uruguay is covered in fertile pasture, supporting millions of sheep and cattle. Wool and woolen products are a major export.

Fray Bentos
Fray Bentos is a large town whose name has been brought to fame by its meatpacking industry.

Paraguay
Landlocked and with few natural resources, Paraguay is largely agricultural. The majority of people are bilingual, speaking Spanish and Guaraní.

Asunción
The full name of Paraguay's capital city is Nuestra Señora Santa María Asunción. It is the country's principal port, situated on the Paraguay River.

Agriculture
The fertile plains of Paraguay are ideal for growing cotton, soybeans, and other crops for export.

Itaipú Dam
The Itaipú Dam on the Paraná River covers all of Paraguay's energy needs, and even some of Brazil's.

Woven bags
Many Guaraní and Macá Amerindians of the vast Gran Chaco region make a living by selling woven bags to tourists.

Andes Mountains
Running the length of Chile along the border with Bolivia and Argentina, the Andes account for more than 80 percent of the country's landscape.

Punta Arenas
Chile's Punta Arenas is the most southerly city in the world and sits underneath the hole in the ozone layer. So, beware the dangerous rays of the Sun!

Angry Earth
Chile has more than 620 volcanoes, many of them active, and the country is also affected by strong earthquakes.

Fruitful valleys
The valleys in the center of Chile produce world-class vines for making wine, as well as fruit, tobacco, and other crops.

Top trains
In 1857, the first railway line opened in Argentina, which soon boasted one of the world's largest rail networks.

Argentina
Traditionally agricultural, the second largest country in South America stretches 2,290 miles (3,694-km) from the Gran Chaco region in the north to the island of Tierra del Fuego in the south.

Chile
Oddly shaped Chile is 2,610 miles (4,200km) long and only 112 miles (180km) wide. This elongated country has a hot desert in the north, glaciers in the south, and a Mediterranean-style climate in the center.

Atacama Desert
The Atacama Desert is rich in minerals, including copper, of which Chile is the world's largest exporter.

Twice as good
Unlike most countries, Bolivia has not one but two capital cities, La Paz and Sucre.

Pampas
Vast grassy plains called the Pampas, used for growing cereals and raising cattle, cover much of central Argentina, where gauchos or cowboys tend the cattle.

Tango
Originating in the slums of Buenos Aires in the late 1800s, the tango is now the national dance of Argentina.

Patagonia
In the south of Argentina lies Patagonia, a largely agricultural area with small communities of former Welsh settlers.

Mt. Aconcagua, Argentina
Highest mountain in South America

La Paz
Highest capital city in the world

Coffee beans

Copacabana Beach

This is the life.

Hooray for Brazil!

Millions of Brazilians!

Ur a swell guy.

Hey, there's mate.

Where's the beef?

They're looking sheepish.

Yee-ha!

Moo

It takes two to tango.

It can be chilly in Chile.

INCA Trail

Asado

Highest mountain in South America

It's all downhill from here.

Have you seen Andy?

I'm not for sale.

Hi!

Hiya!

Hot stuff!

Sucre

Don't have two presidents?

This is nuts.

I'm full of beans.

Buckling plates

As one tectonic plate hits another, it buckles and throws up a huge mountain chain, such as the Himalayas in central Asia. Because the plates are constantly moving, this process never ends—the Himalayas continue to rise by about 0.2in (5mm) each year.

Mountains thrust upward.

Moving plates

Don't buckle under pressure.

Fractured Earth

As Earth's tectonic plates knock into or slide past each other, they often put the rocks under such strain that they crack or fracture into faults. This allows the blocks of rock to move up, down, or sideways against each other along these faults.

This one's faulty.

Fault line

Blocks moving in opposite directions along the fault

I feel shaky.

I'm quaking in my boots!

This is shocking.

Shock waves

Shaky Earth

Tectonic plates usually slide past each other with little problem, but occasionally the plates get stuck. The forces pushing the plates then build up until the rocks give way, resulting in a sudden movement of the plates that sends out shock waves, or vibrations, through the ground—an earthquake.

This is your fault.

Now, focus!

Fault line, where the two plates meet

Focus of earthquake

Did you feel something?

My hardhat blew off!

Exploding Earth

Volcanoes are gaps in Earth's crust through which magma (hot, molten rock) and ash are flung across the surface, forced out by a buildup of gases underground, in what can be spectacularly violent eruptions.

Volcano built up from layers of lava and ash

Ashes to ashes...

Main volcanic pipe or vent

Branch pipe

Magma chamber

I'm feeling gassy.

Rock cycle

As Earth has evolved over millions of years, three main types of rock have formed in its crust: igneous rocks formed as molten magma solidified, metamorphic rocks were transformed by heat or pressure, while sedimentary rocks are compacted debris that settled on the ocean floor millions of years ago.

Rock and roll

Yikes!

A landslide!

You've got rocks in your head.

17

SOUTH AMERICA

The triangle-shaped continent of South America is the fourth largest in size. The towering Andes mountains stretch the length of its Pacific coast from Colombia in the north to the tip of Chile and Argentina in the south. To the east of the Andes lie the massive and luscious Amazon rain forest, and the grassy Gran Chaco and Pampas regions.

(Aaargh!)

Amazon River

The Amazon River rises in the Andes and, after a lengthy journey of about 4,000 miles (6,400km), tips itself into the Atlantic Ocean. It carries more water than the Nile (the longest river in the world), has the largest drainage basin of any river anywhere, and is so wide that not a single bridge crosses over it.

Km
Miles

It's off the charts!

Very Wide

Ain't no river wide enough...

Amazon rain forest

Almost the entire Amazon River basin is covered in the largest tropical rain forest in the world. One-fifth of all the world's species of birds lives here, as well as 2.5 million insect species, 2,000 different mammals, and many thousands of different types of trees and plants.

Very lush

Boo!

Can I order some books here?

There's something fishy about this.

Is that a leak?

What leak?

Amazon

A balmy palm

Grrrr.

Georgetown, GUYANA

Paramaribo, SURINAME

Cayenne, FRENCH GUIANA

Guiana Highlands

Amazon basin

Caracas, VENEZUELA

Llanos

Orinoco

Bogotá, COLOMBIA

Quito, ECUADOR

Lima, PERU

La Paz, BOLIVIA

Equator

Angel Falls

Named after American pilot Jimmy Angel who spotted the falls in 1935, water from the Auyantepui plateau in Venezuela falls 3,212ft (979m) into the Churún River below. Its greatest single drop of 2,648ft (807m) is the highest uninterrupted waterfall in the world.

This is heavenly.

Very high

Lake Titicaca

The world's highest navigable lake, Lake Titicaca is 12,507ft (3,812m) above sea level. It lies on the border

...world's major producers of tin, as well as gold, silver, iron, zinc, and magnesium, among other minerals.

highest capital city, golf course, ski run, and soccer stadium. About 70 percent of the people are Quechua or Aymara Amerindians, while the rest are European descendants or of mixed race.

Lake Titicaca

Despite being landlocked, Bolivia has a naval force, which uses Lake Titicaca for naval exercises.

Llamas

Relied on as pack animals, llamas are also bred for their wool, meat, and their droppings are used as fuel.

descendants of the Incas who ruled the region 400 years ago. Others are mestizo (mixed race), and a few are of European descent. The country is rich in mineral resources and is mainly agricultural.

Potatoes

The original Inca peoples of Peru were the first people to grow potatoes, drying them to produce flour for making bread.

One potato, two potato...

I'm Mr. Potato Head.

Fishing industry

The cool coastal waters of Peru teem with plankton, which provide food for huge numbers of anchovies, sardines, and mackerel.

Holy mackerel!

Aaargh!

Mangrove swamps

The saltwater mangrove swamps on the coast support millions of shrimp, which are now farmed for export.

High train

At 15,885ft (4,843m) above sea level, Peru has the highest railway track in the world.

Otovalo wool

High in the Andes, the Otovalo Amerindians weave llama and alpaca wool to make woolen goods for selling.

Woolly bully!

Lonesome George

The aptly named Lonesome George is the last remaining Abingdon Island tortoise, native to the offshore Galapagos Islands.

Take your time, George.

Ecuador

Named after the Equator, which cuts through it, Ecuador consists of coastal lowlands which are separated by the Andes Mountains. After a major economic crisis from 1998 to 1999 the country began using the U.S. dollar.

Those dollars make cents.

Bananas

Ecuador is one of the world's largest producers of bananas, growing them on the fertile coastal plains.

They're going bananas.

Panama hat

Made from the leaves of the jipijapa plant, Panama hats are actually made in Ecuador for export to Panama.

Hats off to you!

Colombia

Colombia is one of the richest countries in South America, with quantities of gold, emeralds, vast energy reserves, and a climate that supports two crops a year.

Emeralds

Mines near Colombia's capital, Bogotá, produce more than half the world's emeralds, which are considered the finest in the world.

You're a gem.

Coffee

Traditionally, coffee has always been an important export for Colombia. Today, it is still one of the world's largest coffee exporters.

Coffee anyone?

Quinoa

Quinoa—a protein-rich cereal that was important in pre-Colombian civilizations—is grown high up in the Andes. Incas called Quinoa the "mother of all seeds."

I've got to seed.

Do I do I smell gas?

I'm full of energy.

Resourceful lands

With massive reserves of coal, oil, and natural gas, Colombia is almost self-sufficient in energy.

Dance the Cumbia

Many Colombians dance the Cumbia—a dance based on a blend of traditions from its past cultures.

Do you Cumbia often?

Venezuela

When Italian explorer Amerigo Vespucci first visited the area in 1499, he named the land Venezuela, or "Little Venice." Today it is a wealthy country due to its immense oil and mineral reserves, and is very urbanized, with 90 percent of its people living in cities.

What a strange bunch.

Caracas

Heavily populated, Venezuela's capital city is now a major financial and commercial center.

We're rich!

Mineral wealth

Venezuela has vast mineral reserves of coal, iron, bauxite, and gold.

Any more pearls of wisdom?

Pearly whites

First heavily fished by the Spanish in the 1500s, the oysters of Venezuela's Pearl Coast are today greatly depleted.

The world's your oyster!

Rain forest tribes

The Yanomami are a native people of hunters and gatherers who live in enormous thatched circular huts called yanos.

$E = mc^2$

ANGEL FALLS

Okay, halo there.

Can't see any falling angels.

The Guianas

The Guiana coast was colonized by the British, Dutch, and French. Former British Guiana is now independent Guyana. Dutch Guiana is now independent Suriname, while French Guiana remains as the only European colony left on the South American mainland.

Swampy rivers

The coastal regions of the Guianas are humid, swampy, and low-lying—ideal for growing rice, sugar cane, and other tropical products.

Suriname

Dutch influence is still evident in the capital city, Paramaribo, which boasts many Dutch-style buildings.

This is a stylish building.

Guyana

The British took control of the country in 1814 and concentrated on growing sugar. Today, it remains famous for its Demerara sugar.

One lump or two?

French Guiana

The European Space Agency launches its Ariane rockets from Kourou on the north coast of French Guiana.

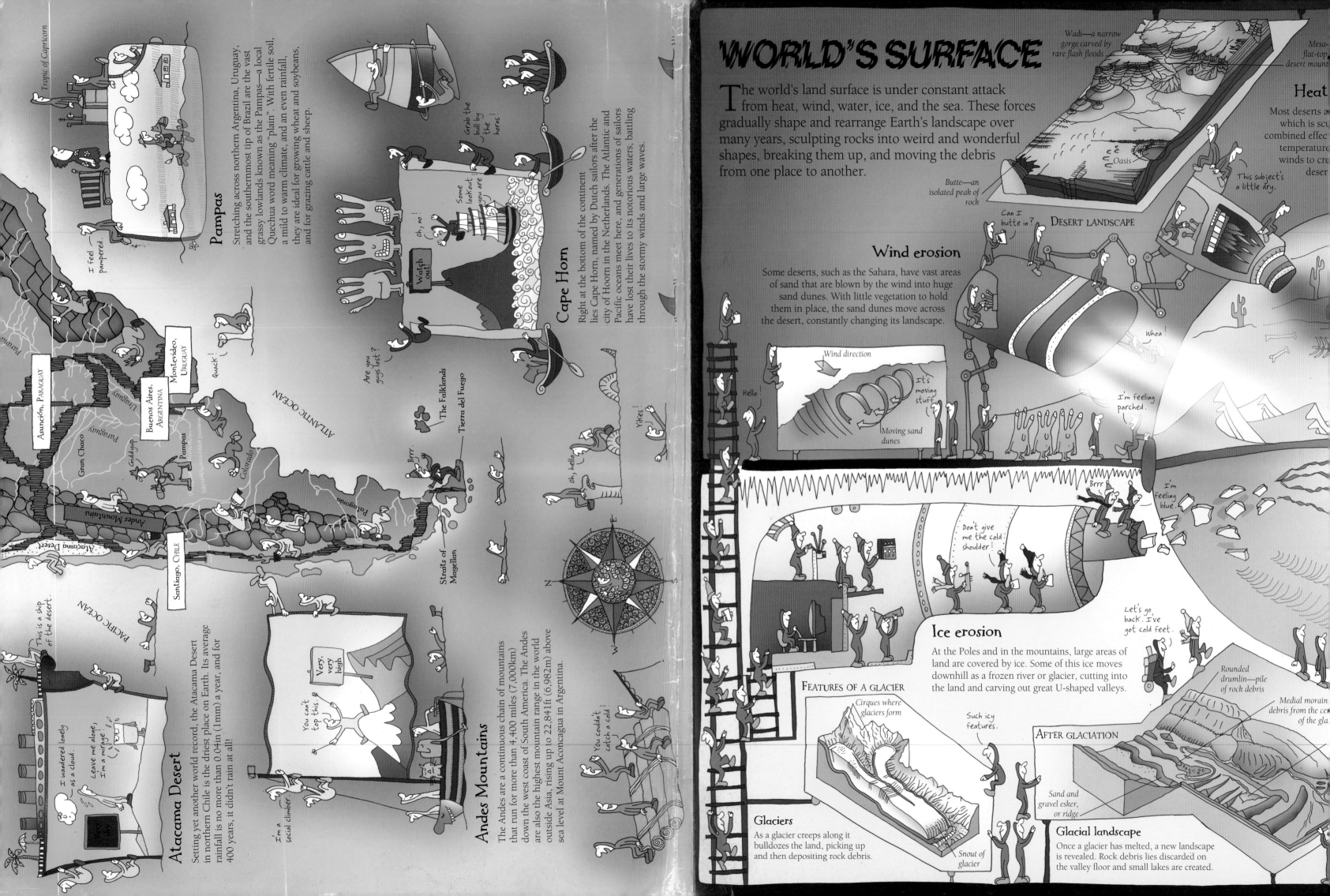

Pampas

Stretching across northern Argentina, Uruguay, and the southernmost tip of Brazil are the vast grassy lowlands known as the Pampas—a local Quechua word meaning "plain". With fertile soil, a mild to warm climate, and an even rainfall, they are ideal for growing wheat and soybeans, and for grazing cattle and sheep.

Cape Horn

Right at the bottom of the continent lies Cape Horn, named by Dutch sailors after the city of Hoorn in the Netherlands. The Atlantic and Pacific oceans meet here, and generations of sailors have lost their lives to its notorious waters, battling through the stormy winds and large waves.

Atacama Desert

Setting yet another world record, the Atacama Desert in northern Chile is the driest place on Earth. Its average rainfall is no more than 0.04in (1mm) a year, and for 400 years, it didn't rain at all!

Andes Mountains

The Andes are a continuous chain of mountains that run for more than 4,400 miles (7,000km) down the west coast of South America. The Andes are also the highest mountain range in the world outside Asia, rising up to 22,841ft (6,982m) above sea level at Mount Aconcagua in Argentina.

Tropic of Capricorn

I feel pampered.

Quack!

Asunción, PARAGUAY
Montevideo, URUGUAY
Buenos Aires, ARGENTINA
Santiago, CHILE

Paraguay
Gran Chaco
Paraguay
Colorado
Pampas
Patagonia
Andes Mountains
Atacama Desert

ATLANTIC OCEAN
PACIFIC OCEAN

The Falklands
Tierra del Fuego
Straits of Magellan

Brrr.
oh, hello.
Yikes!
Are you guys lost?

Grab the bull by the horns!
Some lookout you are!
oh, no!
Watch out!

This is a ship of the desert.
I wandered lonely as a cloud.
Leave me alone, I'm a mirage.
I'm a social climber.
You can't top this.
Very, very high
You couldn't catch a cold!

WORLD'S SURFACE

The world's land surface is under constant attack from heat, wind, water, ice, and the sea. These forces gradually shape and rearrange Earth's landscape over many years, sculpting rocks into weird and wonderful shapes, breaking them up, and moving the debris from one place to another.

Wadi—a narrow gorge carved by rare flash floods

Mesa—flat-top desert mount

Heat

Most deserts a which is sc combined effec temperature winds to cre deser

This subject's a little dry.

Oasis

Butte—an isolated peak of rock

DESERT LANDSCAPE

Can I butte in?

Wind erosion

Some deserts, such as the Sahara, have vast areas of sand that are blown by the wind into huge sand dunes. With little vegetation to hold them in place, the sand dunes move across the desert, constantly changing its landscape.

Wind direction
It's moving stuff
Moving sand dunes

Hello.

Whoa!

I'm feeling parched.

Brrr

I'm feeling blue.

Don't give me the cold shoulder!

Let's go back. I've got cold feet.

Ice erosion

At the Poles and in the mountains, large areas of land are covered by ice. Some of this ice moves downhill as a frozen river or glacier, cutting into the land and carving out great U-shaped valleys.

FEATURES OF A GLACIER

Cirques where glaciers form

Such icy features.

Snout of glacier

Rounded drumlin—pile of rock debris

Medial morain debris from the cen of the gla

AFTER GLACIATION

Sand and gravel esker, or ridge

Glaciers

As a glacier creeps along it bulldozes the land, picking up and then depositing rock debris.

Glacial landscape

Once a glacier has melted, a new landscape is revealed. Rock debris lies discarded on the valley floor and small lakes are created.

The first humans originated in Africa 1.7 million years ago and spread out from here to the rest of the world. Today, with 14 percent of the world's population spread across 53 countries, the African continent houses countless different peoples speaking many different languages, living among some of the most spectacularly varied wildlife, vegetation, and scenery on the planet.

The Maghreb

Isolated from the rest of Africa by the Sahara, the countries of the Maghreb are among the richer African nations, helped by tourism in Morocco and Tunisia, and oil and gas in Algeria.

Morocco

The Kingdom of Morocco is famous for its historic towns, such as Fez and Marrakech, and their bustling souks, or markets.

Atlas Mountains

Algeria

Algeria is a major exporter of natural gas to Europe and has reserves of oil, iron ore, and phosphates.

Phosphates

Morocco possesses about one-third of the world's reserves of phosphates, used to make fertilizers.

Tunisia

Popular with Europeans, Tunisia is an alluring destination on the Mediterranean coast for hot beach vacations.

Libya

Located between the Maghreb and Egypt, Libya was once a colony of the Roman Empire.

The ruined Roman town of Leptis Magna

The Nile Valley

A lifeline for the area, with many millions of people living along its banks, the Nile has two main tributaries—the White and Blue Niles—which meet in Sudan, and then flow north through Egypt to the Mediterranean Sea.

Suez Canal

The 100-mile- (160km-) long Suez Canal connects the Mediterranean and Red Seas—a useful route for sailing between Europe and Asia.

Egypt

The legendary Sphinx guards the pyramids of ancient Egypt at Giza.

Sudan

Khartoum, Sudan's capital, sits on the banks of the Nile where its two tributaries meet.

The Nile River

An essential water source for the locals, the Nile is also a major transportation highway.

Sudan's crops

Cotton, gum arabic from Acacia trees, and sesame seeds are just some of Sudan's crops.

The Niger Valley

The Niger River rises in the central highlands of Guinea and flows northeast before taking a sharp turn to head south through Nigeria and empty out into the Gulf of Guinea. The third longest river in Africa, the Niger, like the Nile, provides important transportation links and is an important water source for the countries that line its banks.

Burkina Faso

Humped zebu cattle, goats, sheep, and camels are the main animals kept by Burkina's farmers.

A calabash made from a gourd is carried on the head by Fulani tribesmen in Burkina.

Mali

The Dogons of Mali build distinctive tall, thin houses high up on a cliff for defense purposes.

Mosques in Mali are made of mud.

Mauritania

Lying to the north of the Niger Valley on the Atlantic coast, Mauritania has a major offshore fishing industry.

Niger

Large reserves of uranium, the fuel used to make nuclear power, are mined in Niger.

The Far West

The extreme west of Africa is watered by the Senegal and Gambia rivers and is mainly low-lying, with grasslands in the south and semidesert conditions towards the north.

Cape Verde

Once a Portuguese colony, many of the towns of these offshore islands have colonial-style buildings.

Senegal

Local griots (tribal storytellers) relate stories of past events accompanied by the kora, a 21-stringed instrument with a soundbox made from a gourd.

Gambia

A narrow strip of land on either side of the Gambia River, Gambia is popular with tourists.

Nigeria

Africa's most populated nation and the 10th most populated country in the world, Nigeria is home to many diverse groups of peoples. Approximately 250 different ethnic groups live here, speaking numerous languages, although English—the former colonial language—is the only official language.

Oil wealth

Nigeria is one of Africa's biggest producers of oil and also has reserves of natural gas as well as iron ore, bauxite, coal, and tin.

Benin

A mainly agricultural nation, Benin's people live off the land and catch fish in its rivers or off its narrow coastline.

Togo

This long, thin country is self-sufficient in basic foodstuffs, growing corn, yams, rice, and cassava to eat, and cocoa, coffee, and cotton to export.

The Guinea Coast

Extending from Guinea-Bissau in the west to Cameroon and Equatorial Guinea in the east, the Guinea Coast is low-lying and wooded, with mangrove swamps along the shore. The origin of its name is not clear, but it is thought to come from Jenne—an important 8th-century trading kingdom.

Guinea-Bissau

Cashews, groundnuts, coconuts, and rice are the main crops grown by Guinea-Bissau's farmers, while its main natural resources are fish and timber.

Guinea

More than 30 per cent of the world's bauxite—used to make aluminum—is mined in Guinea, as well as gold, diamonds, and iron ore.

Sierra Leone

Rich in diamonds, Sierra Leone provides many of the gems used in engagement rings and other pieces of jewelry.

Liberia

Founded in 1847 as a home for freed U.S. slaves returning to Africa, Liberia has plantations of rubber trees that are tapped for their latex—the sap that is used to make rubber.

The Ivory and Gold Coasts

These two stretches of the Guinea Coast were named by Europeans for the products they traded there. The region is tropical and fertile, allowing a wide range of crops to be grown.

Ivory Coast

The world's biggest producer of cocoa, the Ivory Coast also exports coffee and timber.

Ghana

Africa's second-biggest producer of gold, Ghana exports this precious metal along with diamonds, bauxite, and manganese.

Copycat building

The massive Roman Catholic basilica of Yamoussoukro is modeled on St. Peter's Basilica in Rome.

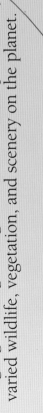

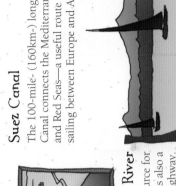
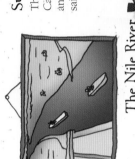

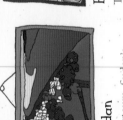

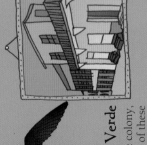
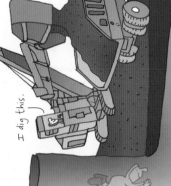

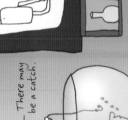

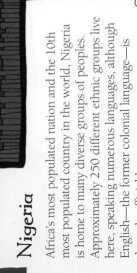

Water erosion

When water falls on the land as rain or snow, it drains into the ground, evaporates into the atmosphere, or runs away into streams and rivers. These rivers cut V-shaped valleys into the landscape, carrying away debris that is eventually deposited at the river's mouth.

Here come the waterworks.

That's a tribute to the river.

Tributary

TYPICAL RIVER VALLEY

Beep beep!

Source of river
What are your sources?

Meander, or bend in the river
This will drive you around the bend.

Delta—an area of deposited sediment, dropped by the river as it slows down and enters the sea

Oxbow lake caused by the river changing its course

Coastal erosion

The sea's waves constantly redesign the shoreline by eroding cliffs and moving sand along beaches. Tides and currents then carry material along the coast, eroding one section while building up another.

Can I borrow a helmet?

I'm surfing.

I'm just coasting.

Strong wave rushes up the beach, carrying sand.

Weak wave carries little sand up the beach.

Weak backwash carries some sand back down the beach.

BUILDING UP THE BEACH

Strong backwash pulls sand off the beach.

ERODING THE BEACH

our support is eroding.

Eroding cliffs

One of the most dramatic results from waves battering the land is when a whole cliff-face collapses into the sea. Along the coastline waves gnaw away at the base of a cliff, gradually undercutting it and causing the unsupported cliff above to collapse under its own weight.

2. Cliff eventually collapses into the sea.

1. Waves undercut the cliff.

Just call me Cliff.

AFRICA

With the world's largest desert, largest river, second-biggest tropical rain forest, and some of the world's biggest lakes, the large continent of Africa is a world-record holder. Sitting on either side of the Equator with a mainly hot climate, Africa contains a wealth of minerals, energy supplies, and other raw materials. African farming has adapted to the uncertainties of the weather from year to year, but at times farming can be difficult due to drought and the encroaching desert.

Watch my river dance.

The Nile

At 4,160 miles (6,695km) long with two main tributaries—the White Nile and the Blue Nile—the Nile is the world's longest river. It floods regularly, depositing vital fertile silt across its floodplain until, that is, the Aswan Dam was erected in southern Egypt, keeping back the river's much-needed silt at the expense of the farmland that lines its route in front of the dam.

I'm parched.

The Sahara

The world's largest desert, the Sahara stretches across almost the whole of North Africa. Thousands of years ago the Sahara had a moist climate, but today wet winds blowing in from the sea are blocked by dry winds sweeping out from the desert, keeping the land dry and parched.

Can we borrow an atlas?

Woohoo!

Safari, so good.

Safari, so good.

The Maghreb

A word meaning "west" in Arabic, the term "Maghreb" was coined by the Egyptians to refer to the lands to their west, which include Tunisia, Algeria, and Morocco. The snow-capped peaks of Morocco's Atlas Mountains contrast with the hot desert in the south of the country.

SAFARI PARK THIS WAY

Help!

MEDITERRANEAN SEA

RED SEA

Djibouti, DJIBOUTI

Horn of Africa

Asmara, ERITREA

Lake Tana

Blue Nile

White Nile

Nile

Nubian Desert

Khartoum, SUDAN

Cairo, EGYPT

Aswan Dam

Lake Nasser

Western Desert

Tibesti

Lake Chad

Ndjamena, CHAD

Ahaggar

Niamey, NIGER

Lomé, TOGO

Abuja, NIGERIA

Tunis, TUNISIA

Tripoli, LIBYA

Algiers, ALGERIA

Ouagadougou, BURKINA FASO

Sahel

Sahara

Rabat, MOROCCO

Atlas Mountains

Gao, MALI

Bamako, MALI

Laâyoune, WESTERN SAHARA (occupied by Morocco)

Tropic of Cancer

Senegal

Nouakchott, MAURITANIA

Dakar, SENEGAL

Praia, CAPE VERDE

Banjul, GAMBIA

Bissau, GUINEA BISSAU

Conakry, GUINEA

Extending from the hot, dry Sahara in the north down to the hot, wet, tropical rain forests of Cameroon and Gabon in the south, Central Africa has extensive oil and mineral reserves and some striking wildlife.

Chad

Chad shares its name with the shrinking lake where Cameroon, Niger, Nigeria, and Chad all meet. Due to serious droughts, Lake Chad today is just a tenth of its original size.

SHRINKING LAKE CHAD

Central African Republic

Landlocked with few roads and no railways, the Central African Republic largely relies on the Ubang River as its main transportation link, which flows along the southern border of the country to join the Congo River.

Equatorial Guinea

This tiny country is mainly tropical rain forest and consists of five offshore islands and a rectangle of land between Cameroon and Gabon.

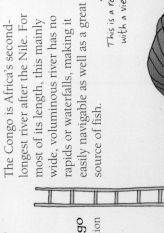

Sao Tome and Principe

Largely volcanic, this two-island republic depends on cocoa exports for almost all its income.

...untouched tropical rain forest, and huge national parks have been set up to protect this important habitat.

The Congo Valley

The Congo is Africa's second-longest river after the Nile. For most of its length, this mainly wide, voluminous river has no rapids or waterfalls, making it easily navigable as well as a great source of fish.

This is a room with a view!

Democratic Republic of Congo

This vast, tropical nation has massive mineral wealth, with large quantities of coltan, which is essential for the production of mobile phones.

Congo

The smaller and more northern of the two nations that share a name, Congo is home to some extraordinary wildlife, including the immense Giant African Snail, which can grow up to 13in (33cm) long.

Horn of Africa

So-named because it is shaped like an animal's horn, the Horn of Africa is the easternmost part of the continent's mainland, jutting out into the Indian Ocean. It is largely desert, although Ethiopia and Eritrea are both mountainous.

Hello? Can you hear me now?

Ciao!

Eritrea

Asmara, Eritrea's capital, boasts many fine Italian-style modern buildings, built when it was an Italian colony during the 20th century.

Somalia

The Boswellia trees that grow in northern Somalia are an important source of frankincense—a resin used to make expensive incense and perfume.

Smells lovely.

Ethiopia

One of the oldest Christian nations on Earth, Ethiopia possesses 11 remarkable cross-shaped churches, each cut out of the solid rock and dating back to the 1200s.

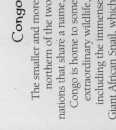

Djibouti

Unusually, Djibouti is named after its capital city, which is a major port in the Red Sea.

East Africa

The five nations of East Africa boast some of the finest wildlife in Africa, with massive game reserves that attract tourists from all around the world.

Where's the monkey wrench?

Kenya

Thousands of tourists visit Kenya each year to view the spectacular array of wild animals in their natural habitats.

This is wild!

Uganda

To help boost fish stocks and provide sport for Uganda's tourists, Nile perch were introduced into Lake Victoria. Unfortunately, they ate all the other fish and are now simply a great menace! That's one fiendish fish.

Central Southern Africa

A broad, grassy plain with tropical forests to the north runs from Angola on the Atlantic coast across to Mozambique on the Indian Ocean. The land is rich enough to provide food for all and teems with wildlife, some of which is protected in game reserves and national parks.

We've got a wealth of options!

Angola

Massive reserves of oil, diamonds, and other minerals provide much of Angola's wealth.

Zimbabwe

In the Bantu language, Zimbabwe means "stone houses" and gets its name from the stone buildings of Great Zimbabwe—an ancient trading city.

Rwanda

One of the mountain gorilla's last refuges is Rwanda's Volcanoes National Park.

Burundi

Fertile land is scarce in Burundi, so most farmers work small plots of land that are just big enough to feed a family.

Southern Africa

The region of southern Africa is dominated by South Africa, which has some of the continent's richest natural resources, notably minerals such as gold and diamonds, and is the richest and most developed economy in Africa. The other countries that make up this area are largely agricultural, with much fertile farmland and pasture.

Tanzania

Fossilized remains of the earliest humans were found in Tanzania's Olduvai Gorge—proof that the first humans lived in Africa.

Mt. Kilimanjaro

Botswana

The Tswana people of Botswana traditionally live in thatched huts arranged around a courtyard.

I've got sand in my shoes!

I'm an armchair explorer.

Namibia

Although it is by the sea, the Namib Desert is hot and dry with some of the biggest sand dunes in the world.

South Africa

The massive Kruger National Park has more than 130 different species of mammal, including the "big five"; lions, African buffalo, leopards, rhinoceroses, and elephants.

Tourism

The beautiful city of Cape Town, at the very tip of Africa, is dominated by Table Mountain.

Lesotho

The lofty lands of Lesotho are all above 3,300ft (1,000m).

Swaziland

The Kingdom of Swaziland relies on sugar, cane as its main export.

Mozambique

Mozambique has some of the best unspoiled beaches in Africa, as well as many national parks.

Zambia

The Zambezi River forms the natural boundary between Zambia and Zimbabwe, dropping a spectacular 420ft (128m) over the magnificent Victoria Falls.

Malawi

Lake Nyasa accounts for one-fifth of the area of Malawi, and is home to many brightly colored fish that are exported to aquariums around the world.

Seychelles

Tourists from around the world are seduced by the Seychelles' beaches, scenery, and climate.

She sells Seychelles...

Mauritius

Unique to Mauritius, the flightless dodo was hunted to extinction.

Don't say it!

Comoros

One of the main crops on the Comoros islands is vanilla, used to flavor ice cream and cakes.

You're as dead as a...

Madagascar

The world's fourth largest island, Madagascar is home to an unusual range of wildlife, including the lemur, which is found nowhere else in the world.

The Indian Ocean

Separated from mainland Africa, the islands of the Indian Ocean have a unique array of wildlife. Most people live off the land or sea, and tourism has become important to the smaller islands.

No man is an island!

I love wildlife programs.

I'm just going with the flow.

That's a serious situation.

Heavily wooded Cameroon boasts quality hardwoods, such as ebony, mahogany, and teak, which are greatly sought after by Western furniture-makers.

What's that monkey's business?

Left page — Africa map

City labels: Lake Turkana, Mogadishu, SOMALIA; Victoria, SEYCHELLES; Nairobi, KENYA; Moroni, COMOROS; Dodoma, TANZANIA; Antananarivo, MADAGASCAR; Port Louis, MAURITIUS; Lake Nyasa; Lilongwe, MALAWI; Maputo, MOZAMBIQUE; Mbabane, SWAZILAND; Maseru, LESOTHO; Harare, ZIMBABWE; Lusaka, ZAMBIA; Lake Tanganyika; Lake Victoria; Kampala, UGANDA; Kigali, RWANDA; Bujumbura, BURUNDI; Gaborone, BOTSWANA; Tshwane/Pretoria, SOUTH AFRICA; Bloemfontein, SOUTH AFRICA; Drakensberg; Cape Town, SOUTH AFRICA; Windhoek, NAMIBIA; Luanda, ANGOLA; Brazzaville, CONGO; Libreville, GABON; Kinshasa, DEMOCRATIC REPUBLIC OF CONGO; Yaoundé, CAMEROON; Malabo, EQUATORIAL GUINEA; São Tomé, SÃO TOME & PRÍNCIPE; Namib Desert; Okavango Delta; Kalahari Desert; Orange River; Congo Basin; Congo; Zambezi; Limpopo; Equator; Tropic of Capricorn; INDIAN OCEAN; ATLANTIC OCEAN

Great Rift Valley

The Great Rift Valley was formed millions of years ago by the pulling apart of two of the plates that form Earth's crust. The valley, which stretches for more than 4,350 miles (7,000km) from Syria in Asia to Mozambique in Africa, contains many beautiful lakes and sheer, steep-sided valleys.

Kalahari Desert

Africa's second largest desert, the Kalahari in the continent's south is a harsh environment that is home to the San—one of the few remaining groups of hunter-gatherers in the world. A marshy swamp—the Okavango Delta—in the desert's north is fed by the Okavango River, which flows inland and eventually evaporates in the intense heat.

The Congo River Basin

The Congo River rises in the mountains of East Africa and eventually flows west in a huge arc before pouring out into the Atlantic Ocean. The river drains a huge area of central Africa, creating a large, wet basin that contains the world's second largest tropical rain forest.

The Sahel

To the south of the Sahara is a semidesert area known as the Sahel. This land is used by farmers to graze their animals but suffers from frequent droughts and soil erosion, causing parts of the Sahel to become more desertlike as the Sahara's sands encroach on the area.

Scale: Km 100 200 300 400 500 600 700 800 900 1000 / Miles 100 200 300 400 500 600 700 800 900 1000

Compass: N E S W

Right page

WEATHER & CLIMATE

An area's weather is what happens from day to day. It can be unpredictable and change quickly, whereas climate is defined by the typical weather recorded in an area for a period of 30 years or more. Climate is affected by latitude, height above sea level, the region's prevailing wind, and the circulation of ocean currents that warm or cool the air around them.

Solar energy

As the Sun's rays bea[m] through Earth's atmo[sphere] toward the ground, [...] more than half their [...] which remains in the [...] or is reflected back i[...]

- 16% absorbed by water vapor and gases in the air
- 7% diffused in the atmosphere
- 27% reflected by clouds
- 3% absorbed by clouds
- 4% reflected by land and oceans
- 24% absorbed by the ground

Greenhouse effect

Gases in Earth's atmosphere trap the Sun's heat, just like a greenhouse. Some human activity releases more "greenhouse gases" into the atmosphere, increasing the greenhouse effect and affecting Earth's weather, which could result in climate change.

Earth's atmosphere / Solar radiation / Heat escapes into space. / Heat reflected back to Earth / What an effective greenhouse.

Everyday [weather]

Air masses in the atmosphere affect o[ur] weather. As they pass overhead, they [...] unchanging weather. However, wher[e one] collides with another, it causes a [...] weather along the boundary, or front, b[...]

WARM FRONT / COLD FRONT
Clouds form along the warm front.
Cold air mass advances into a warm air mass.
Warm air mass advances into a cold air mass.
Thunderstorms and rain occur along the cold front.

Vegetation zones

Plants and animals vary massively from region to region across Earth, strongly influenced by climate. Scientists have identified nine basic environments known as biomes, each of which has a typical array of plants and animals that have adapted to survive within it.

MOUNTAIN REGIONS / TROPICAL GRASSLAND / TEMPERATE FOREST / POLAR AND TUNDRA / MEDITERRANEAN / DRY GRASSLAND / TAIGA OR COLD FOREST / TROPICAL RAIN FOREST / HOT DESERT

Storms

Severe weather, including strong winds, drivi[ng rain,] and thunder and lightning, is often called a st[orm,] although a storm is scientifically defined as a[...] where winds reach more than 55mph (88k[ph),] Force 10 on the Beaufort scale.

Thunder and lightning

A flash of lightning from an electrically charged thundercloud heats the air and causes it to expand, creating a clap of thunder.

Lightning flashes from a negatively charged to a positively charged area.

Hurricanes

These hugely destructive [...] are a mass of violent tropi[cal...] cluster around a ring of lo[...] over water.

Signs: THIS WAY PLEASE / ENTRANCE / THIS WAY / LOOK UP / This way

Northern Ireland

...untry boasts an array of beautiful scenery, including the dramatic ... Causeway—a group ... columns formed by ... volcanic activity.

...top! You're not ...posed to take ...he ball. It's art!

...Nonsense! ...out my way.

Baa!

Wales

Traditionally livestock farmers, the Welsh are passionate about rugby, which is their national game.

Ireland

The island Republic of Ireland lies to the west of the UK. Famous for its traditional folk music and a long line of distinguished poets, playwrights, and authors, Ireland is a very fertile country with major food processing and high-tech industries.

I'm jockeying for position.

Horse training

Ireland is world-famous for its breeding and training of some of the best racehorses.

Guinness

A dark, dry stout beer, Guinness is one of the national drinks of Ireland.

Quoi? *Eat my dust!*

Tour de France

Every year, cyclists take to the roads to compete in the Tour de France, watched by thousands of eager spectators.

France

The largest country in western Europe, France is famed for its fine foods and wines, an inspiring fashion industry, its historic chateaux or grand houses, and some of the most stunning countryside.

SKIING IN THE FRENCH ALPS

Wine

French vineyards produce a wide range of quality wines that are exported around the world.

Cheers, mon amis

Eiffel Tower

Named after its designer, Gustave Eiffel, and erected in 1889 to mark the centenary of the French Revolution, the Eiffel Tower dominates the Paris skyline.

Voila

Monaco

The tiny principality of Monaco lies on the Mediterranean coast. Every year, Formula 1 cars race around its narrow streets during the Grand Prix.

This is grand. *A winning formula*

Scotland

One of Scotland's famous and most recognized traditions is the wearing of the kilt by Scotsmen.

...highland cattle ...d red deer are ...on sights in the ...tish Highlands.

Do my knees look big in this?

ENGLISH PLAYWRIGHT WILLIAM SHAKESPEARE

The United Kingdom

The countries that make up the UK are all ruled over by the same monarch. While being different in culture and character, all four share a common language, government, and currency.

England

Tourists flock to the UK's capital, London, to visit such famous structures as the London Eye and Big Ben.

Sardines

The main catch of Portuguese fishermen is sardines, a local delicacy.

Two heads are better than one.

THE ALHAMBRA PALACE AND FORTRESS IN GRANADA, BUILT BY THE ISLAMIC MOORS

Spain

The south of Spain was once occupied by the Islamic Moors, who left behind many beautiful buildings.

The Iberian Peninsula

Across the Pyrenees Mountains from France lies the Iberian Peninsula, a largely rocky region between the Atlantic Ocean and Mediterranean Sea, occupied by Spain and Portugal.

Portugal

Produced from grapes grown in the north of the country and stored in casks, or "pipes," made from the local oak trees before bottling, port is Portugal's most famous export.

This is the first port of call.

Andorra

This tiny nation is unique in having two joint heads of state—the President of France and the Bishop of Urgell in Spain.

Modern art

The strikingly modern Guggenheim Museum in Bilbao, Spain, designed by Frank Gehry, attracts thousands of tourists.

Flamenco dancing originated in 15th-century Andalucia.

The Low Countries

The low-lying nations of Belgium, the Netherlands, and Luxembourg—their joint names often abbreviated to Benelux—are among the richest nations in Europe and are very crowded, with most people living in the many historic towns and cities.

Belgium

The Belgian capital, Brussels, is a truly international city since it is also capital of the EU.

Are these french fries or Belgian fries?

Luxembourg

The tiny duchy of Luxembourg has three official languages—French, German, and Luxembourgish—and is a major international banking center.

The Netherlands

With one-quarter of its land below sea level and four major rivers running through it, the Netherlands is kept high and dry by a massive system of dykes and drainage canals.

Baltics

...three Baltic states are ...y flat, wooded, and ...ltural, although they are ...ping high-tech industries. ...7, Estonia became the first ...ry in the world to hold ...onal Internet election.

Latvia

Fertile soils and a flat landscape make Latvia ideal for farming, particularly dairy cattle and pigs.

Lithuania

Baltic amber—the fossilized resin of conifer trees—is world-famous and is used to make jewelry.

Does this look wooden?

Pine forests provide timber for houses and furniture, and wood-pulp for paper.

Estonia

Tallinn, Estonia's capital, is an important seaport and high-tech center with a beautiful medieval Old Town.

I see the cow has come home.

Rotterdam

Located within the delta of the Rhine and Meuse rivers, Rotterdam is Europe's largest and busiest port.

...ople herd reindeer ... Norway, ..., and Finland.

This bridges a gap.

What are the rates for the summer?

Denmark

The Øresund bridge between Denmark and Sweden is the longest combined road-and-rail bridge in Europe.

Sweden

Each winter, the Torne River's frozen waters are used to make an ice hotel, which then melts during the spring thaw.

The stave churches of Norway and Sweden are made from wood—a common building material.

Norway

Norway's mountainous countryside is ideal for producing hydroelectricity, while North Sea oil makes the country self-sufficient in fuel.

Germany

The most populous country in Europe aside from Russia, stretching from the North Sea to the Alps, Germany is Europe's major economic and industrial power.

That's one fine Rhine.

RIVER RHINE

Finland

...cent years Finland ...has developed its ...gh-tech industries, ...ing Nokia mobile ...s and other items.

LITTLE MERMAID STATUE, COPENHAGEN HARBOR, DENMARK

Offshore wind farms provide one-fifth of Denmark's electricity.

This puts a spring in my step.

Poland

A large, mainly low-lying country at the heart of Europe, Poland has major shipbuilding, electronic, and steel industries, although about a quarter of the workforce is employed on the land.

Religion

The Poles are devout Roman Catholics, and many Catholics make a pilgrimage to the shrine of the Black Madonna at Czestochowa, which was painted by St. Luke the Evangelist. Legend has it that the painting protects the city.

EUROVISION ART SHOW

... treasure-trove of art and historic buildings, diverse cultures ...nd peoples, Europe's 44 independent countries include the ...d's smallest and largest. Many of these nations are members ...e European Union (EU)—an economic and political union ...nded in 1957 that now covers most of western, ...ral, and southern Europe.

Iceland

About one-tenth of volcanic Iceland is covered with glaciers. There are also many hot springs.

Scandinavia

The five prosperous Scandinavian countries in the north of Europe have much common history and culture between them, forging close links to work together on issues of common concern.

Is it ready? *There's still a couple of bugs.*

Engineering

Germany is famed for its engineering, producing superb machines, such as steadfast cars, and industrial products.

Mad castles

Legendary King Ludwig II of Bavaria built three extraordinary, fairy-tale castles in the hills of southern Germany.

FRANKFURTER SAUSAGES AND SAUERKRAUT

Sweet wheat

Toy boat, toy boat, toy boat...

GDANSK SHIPYARD

ENTER

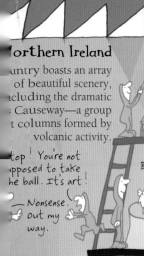
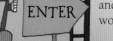

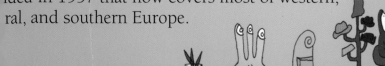

THE BEAUFORT SCALE

0: Calm	4: Moderate wind	8: Gale
1: Light air	5: Fresh breeze	9: Strong gale
2: Light breeze	6: Strong breeze	10: Storm
3: Gentle breeze	7: Near gale	11: Violent storm
		12: Hurricane

This is a breeze.

0: CALM
0–1MPH
(0–2KPH)

4: MODERATE BREEZE
13–18MPH
(20–29KPH)

8: GALE
39–46MPH
(62–74KPH)

12: HURRICANE MORE THAN 73MPH (117KPH)

Aaargh!

Help!

North Pole

Cold air

Equator

Warm air

THIS WAY

Clouds form as water condenses, and rain and snow fall on land.

Winds

As air moves between hot and cold regions, it causes a change in air pressure, which creates wind. Winds move from areas of high pressure (where the air is cold) to areas of low pressure (where it is warmer). The strength of the wind is measured by the 13-point Beaufort Scale.

Water evaporates from lakes, rivers, and vegetation.

I'm on Cloud Nine!

Rain falls over oceans.

Water runs off into the sea.

Water evaporates from oceans.

Talk about running water.

THIS WAY

Wind circulation

As Earth rotates it causes the world's winds to circulate. This global corkscrew of circulating air moves warm air from the Equator to the Poles, and cold air in the opposite direction, thus maintaining a balance of temperatures around the world.

Do you feel a draft?

Water cycle

The air around us is always moist since it contains invisible water vapor. If the air is cooled, this vapor condenses into water and circulates between Earth and the atmosphere in a neverending cycle—evaporating in the heat and returning as rain or snow in the cold.

THIS WAY

This is clouding my thinking...

Cirrus

Cirrostratus

Cirrocumulus

Cumulonimbus

Altocumulus

Altostratus

Nimbostratus

Stratocumulus

Cumulus

Stratus

Got your head in the clouds again!

THIS WAY

Help!

Tornadoes

Tornadoes form below thunderclouds as whirling windstorms, and can bring devastating winds of up to 250mph (400kph).

Fog

Low-lying clouds of water droplets, known as fog, form when warm, moist air is cooled by the ground below. However, fog can also form on cold, calm nights, as heat absorbed by the ground during the day radiates back into the air, causing the air to heat up but then cool quickly to form fog.

Clouds

When water vapor in the air is lifted high up in the sky, it cools and condenses into a cloud. There are 10 basic types of clouds, which form at different heights in the atmosphere, and hardly a day goes by when there isn't a cloud in the sky.

EUROPE

Europe is the world's second-smallest continent, yet it packs in 44 separate countries, including two—Turkey and the Russian Federation—that straddle the border with Asia. The continent is densely packed, with most people living in the crowded towns and cities. Its land is generally fertile, although broken up in places by imposing mountain ranges and great rivers.

Has anyone seen my hat?

Brrr...

Scandinavia

The cold, northern European countries Norway, Denmark, and Sweden together Scandinavia, although the term is usuall to include both Finland and Iceland, to both Sweden and Finland are low-lying many lakes and forests, Norway is mountainous, Iceland volcanic, and Denmark flat and very fertile.

Reykjavik, ICELAND

Got any oil?

Go fish!

Faeroe Islands (to Denmark)

NORWEGIAN SEA

NORTH SEA

Olso, NORWAY

Stock S

North Sea

Dividing Britain from mainland Europe, the North Sea was once a rich fishing ground and its basin a massive reservoir of oil and natural gas. Today, overfishing has significantly depleted its fish stocks, and easily accessible reserves of oil and gas are also running out.

Copenhagen, DENMARK

Amsterdam, NETHERLANDS

Shannon

Dublin, IRELAND

London, UK

The Hague

Elbe

Oder

North

ATLANTIC OCEAN

Thames

ENGLISH CHANNEL

Rhine

Berlin, GERMANY

Careful!

Brussels, BELGIUM

Luxembourg, LUXEMBOURG

Prague, CZECH REPUBLIC

Vienne AUSTRI

Paris, FRANCE

Seine

Bern, SWITZERLAND

Liechtenstein

Lisbon, PORTUGAL

Loire

Alps

Ljubljana, SLOVENIA

Budapest, HUNGARY

BAY OF BISCAY

Andorra la Vella, ANDORRA

Rhône

Zagreb CROATIA

Sara BOSNI HERZEGO

Alps

The collision of the African and European continents that began 65 million years ago pushed up the Alps and other mountains of southern Europe. The Alps form a natural boundary between North and Mediterranean Europe, but are now traversed by many road and rail tunnels.

San Marino

Apennines

ADRIATIC SEA

Belgra SER

Madrid, SPAIN

Mónaco

Pyrenees

Vatican City

Pod MONT

STRAIT OF GIBRALTAR

Rome, ITALY

MEDITERRANEAN SEA

Need a hand?

Every little bit alps.

Valletta, MALTA

Km	100	200	300	400	500	600	700
0							
Miles	100	200	300	400	500	600	700

...and Bulgaria

...d Bulgaria are Orthodox ...nations and both use ... script to write ... the Latin script ...o most other ...countries.

...picturesque.

THE PARTHENON, ATHENS

This is very civilized!

Hooray for me!

Greece

More than 2,500 years ago, Greece was the center of European civilization. Many famous buildings survive from that period.

The Olympics

Ancient Greece was the home of the Olympic Games. Revived in 1896, they were recently hosted by Greece again in 2004.

I like my seas blue.

A rose by any other name...

Bulgarian roses

The petals of Bulgaria's roses are harvested to produce the rose oil used in perfume.

He rose to the occasion.

The Black Sea

Bulgaria's Black Sea coast is a major tourist destination for western Europeans and Russians anxious to enjoy some summer sun.

I'm a man of letters.

Cyprus

Aside from tourism, farming is the mainstay of Cyprus's economy and Cypriots grow olives for their oil, citrus fruit, and grapes.

Mediterranean Islands

The Mediterranean Sea contains two island republics—Malta and Cyprus. The latter is actually located in Asia, but is European in outlook and a member of the EU.

San Marino

The world's oldest republic, San Marino generates most of its income through the sale of postage stamps.

...narrowest point of the ...an between Italy and North ...is an important harbor for ...d naval shipping.

I want all of the olives.

I try to keep a good outlook.

The Swiss Guard—protectors of the Pope.

Vatican City

The world's smallest independent state lies in central Rome. It is ruled by the pope and is the headquarters of the Roman Catholic Church.

I've seen this scene somewhere before.

Italy

Boot-shaped Italy, kicking into the Mediterranean Sea, is renowned for its wealth of beautiful medieval churches and palaces. Its capital, Rome, once commanded a mighty empire that controlled most of western Europe.

I prefer soap operas.

Opera

Originating in Italy in the 16th century, opera is still the country's most popular musical form.

Roman ruins

Italy is brimming with remains from the Roman Empire, including the Colosseum in Rome, where gladiators once fought.

...y rural nation sits across some ...or road and rail links between ...ast Europe, and is attracting ...numbers of tourists to its ...nery.

...e to ...ria for the ...d of music.

WOLFGANG AMADEUS MOZART

Liechtenstein

As asserted in its national anthem, the tiny Principality of Liechtenstein sits on the River Rhine, between Switzerland and Austria.

Switzerland

Timepieces are a major export industry for the Swiss, who are renowned for their precision engineering.

Mountaineering as a sport began in the Swiss Alps.

I'm running late.

The Alps

Four states nestle in the peaks of the Alps—Europe's highest mountain chain—of which Switzerland and Liechtenstein are officially neutral, meaning they are not allied with any other nations.

Austria

The birthplace of Mozart and the Strauss family, Austria is famous for its music, as well as its delectable Sacher Torte chocolate cake.

...ral Europe

...ndlocked central European ...are highly industrialized, making ...ange of manufactured goods ...cars and other machines, as well ...ng much agricultural produce.

Czech glass

The Czech Republic is famous for its quality Bohemian Crystal glassware and decorative arts.

Slovakia

The Tatra Mountains of northern Slovakia are attracting increasing numbers of tourists to their ski resorts.

Hungary

Budapest, the capital of Hungary, was once two cities, with Buda and its magnificent castle on one side of the River Danube and Pest on the other.

Yum!

Goulash soup— Hungary's national dish

Czech Republic

Prague, the Czech capital, is one of ...Europe's most beautiful capital cities, ...sitting on the River Vltava and ...dominated by its historic castle.

The Balkans

With the exception of Albania, the countries of the Balkans are relatively young, having emerged as independent states from 1991 onward. So far, none are members of the EU.

Croatia

The Adriatic coastline of Croatia contains many old towns, such as Dubrovnik, popular with tourists and sailors.

Bosnia

Originally built in 1566 and traditionally used as a diving platform for young men to prove their bravery, Bosnia's famous Mostar Bridge was restored in 1994.

Albania

Known by its people as "the land of the eagles," Albania is largely agricultural with most Albanians working on the land for a living.

Macedonia

The capital, Skopje, of this mountainous, landlocked republic lies in an earthquake zone and has been destroyed four times in its history.

Top spot!

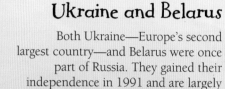

Serbia

The Serbs are Orthodox Christians and share a language with the Croats, although they use different scripts to write it down.

Right on the mark.

ST. MARK'S CHURCH, BELGRADE, SERBIA

Look what's cropped up!

Mine's still an underground phenomenon.

Fifth time's the charm

Montenegro

Montenegro ("Black Mountain") became one of the world's newest states after gaining independence from Serbia in 2006.

Romania and Moldova

Once united as a single country, Romania and Moldova are surrounded by mainly Slav-speaking and Cyrillic-writing states, yet they speak and write a language (Romanian) more like French or Italian.

Moldova

The rich, black soil of Moldova is ideal for growing cotton, grapes, and sunflowers, the seeds of which are a valuable export crop.

Ukraine and Belarus

Both Ukraine—Europe's second largest country—and Belarus were once part of Russia. They gained their independence in 1991 and are largely flat and agricultural, although Ukraine also has substantial heavy industries.

Flower power!

I'm an independent type.

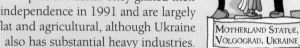

MOTHERLAND STATUE, VOLGOGRAD, UKRAINE

Romania

The Carpathian Mountains separate Transylvania, home of the legendary Count Dracula, from the rest of the country, which lies along the Danube River valley.

SKIING IN THE CARPATHIANS

Kiev

Ukraine's ancient capital was founded in the 9th century. Its most famous landmark is the gold-domed St. Sophia's Cathedral.

Belarus

The Pripet Marshes in southern Belarus are the largest marshlands in Europe and are home to elk and wild boar.

Ukraine

The Donbass basin in eastern Ukraine is Europe's largest coalfield and supports massive iron and steel works, car plants, and other industries.

Don't be a boar.

Come on!

Where's the fire?

I hit my head and saw tsars.

Get to the pointe.

Hello, dolly!

Russian Federation

The largest nation on Earth, Russia stretches across both the European and Asian continents. Most people live in the towns and cities of western Russia.

MATRIOSHKA DOLLS

Russian ballet

Russia is renowned for its ballet companies—the Kirov from St. Petersburg and the Bolshoi from Moscow.

St. Petersburg

The capital of the Russian Empire for 200 years, St. Petersburg was built by Peter the Great in the early 1700s as a "window to the west."

Watch out below!

The Kremlin

A fortified citadel in the heart of Moscow, the Kremlin includes the palace of the former tsars. Today, the Russian government has its headquarters here.

THE WINTER PALACE, ST. PETERSBURG

ST. BASIL'S CATHEDRAL, MOSCOW

EXIT

OCEANS

More than two-thirds of Earth is covered in saltwater, most of which is contained within five great oceans that are home to millions of different fish and marine mammals. Until recently humans knew little about this watery world, but new technology has opened it up to human exploration and discovery.

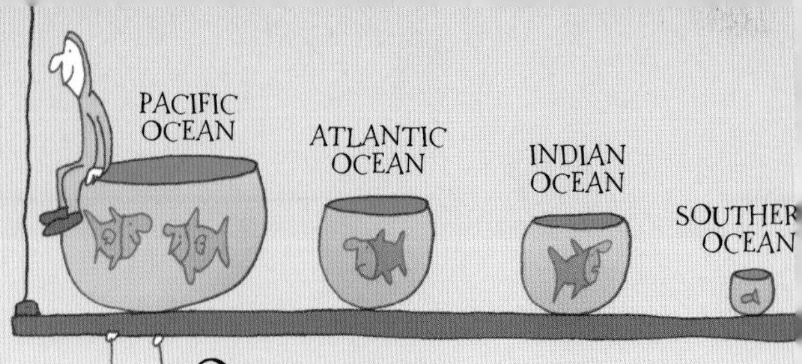

North European Plain

The vast North European Plain stretches the width of the continent from the Fens in England to the Ural Mountains in Russia. The flat, fertile plain never rises more than 1,000ft (300m) above sea level and is used to grow wheat and other crops.

River Danube

One of Europe's longest rivers and an economic lifeline for eastern Europe, the Danube passes through or alongside Germany, Austria, Slovakia, Hungary, Croatia, Serbia, Romania, Bulgaria, Ukraine, and Moldova, often forming a natural border between countries, before emptying out into the Black Sea.

Mediterranean Sea

The popular tourist destination of southern Europe, with its attractively warm climate, lies along the Mediterranean Sea. This almost completely landlocked expanse of water is connected to the Atlantic Ocean through a single narrow channel: the 8-mile- (13km-) wide Strait of Gibraltar.

Ocean sizes

The world's five oceans and many seas occupy 139 million sq miles (361 million sq km) of surface. The Pacific Ocean is biggest in size, colossal 46.4 percent of the total watery surfa

Continental shelf

The edge of each continent slopes down into the sea, forming a shelf of shallow water.

Coral reefs

These underwater tropical forests are formed from the hard outer skeletons of tiny sea creatures called polyps.

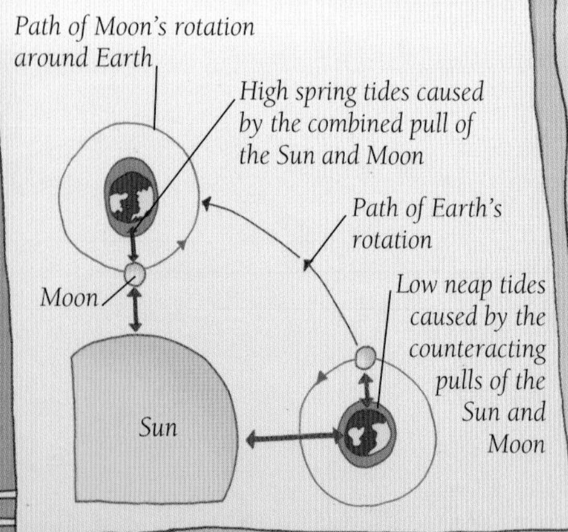

Continental slope

Beyond the continental shelf the ocean floor plunges steeply down the continental slope toward the deepest part of the ocean.

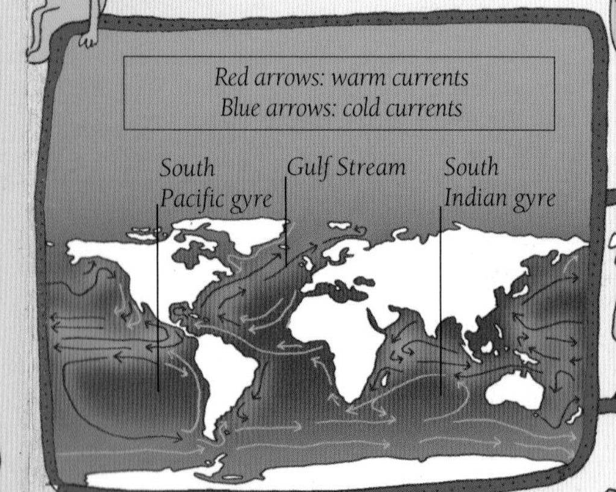

Tides

The gravitational pull between the spinning Earth, Moon, and Sun causes the oceans around the globe to rise and flood the shore, and then fall back, or ebb, again every 12 hours.

Path of Moon's rotation around Earth

High spring tides caused by the combined pull of the Sun and Moon

Path of Earth's rotation

Low neap tides caused by the counteracting pulls of the Sun and Moon

Moon

Sun

Surface currents

The world's winds disturb the surface of the oceans, causing currents that flow in curves, known as gyres, due to Earth's rotation. Warm currents flow away from the Equator; cold currents flow toward it.

Red arrows: warm currents
Blue arrows: cold currents

South Pacific gyre | Gulf Stream | South Indian gyre

Ocean-basin floor

Past the continental shelf, the ocean-basin floor plummets to more than 6,560ft (2,000m) deep. Here, midocean ridges and trenches snake along the ocean floor. Descend even further to 16,400ft (5,000m) and discover the abyssal plain—the deepest, darkest part of the ocean floor, covered in a thick ooze.

Pillow lava

When bubbles of lava erupt from a midocean ridge, they cool and solidify upon contact with the cold seawater, creating pillow-shaped lumps of rock that litter the ocean floor.

Pillow lava

Midocean

As the Earth's plates pull apa ocean floor, m from the Earth form a midocean

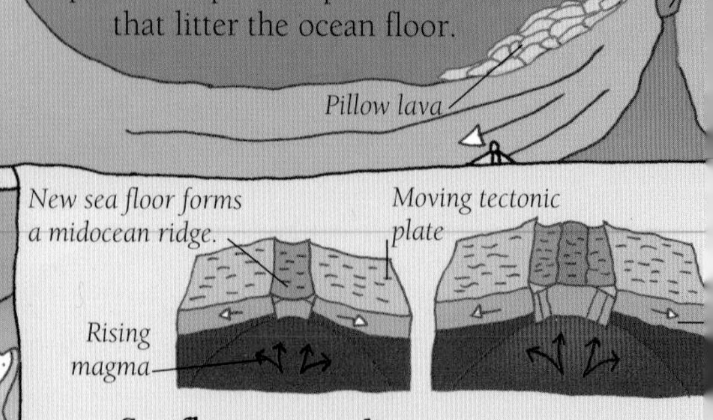

Seafloor spreading

As two plates pull apart, magma rises up between form a ridge. This new seafloor is in turn pushe more magma rising beneath it in a process calle spreading, which is gradually widening the ocea

New sea floor forms a midocean ridge

Moving tectonic plate

Rising magma

PACIFIC OCEAN | ATLANTIC OCEAN | INDIAN OCEAN | SOUTHERN OCEAN

Map labels:
KARA SEA
BARENTS SEA
WHITE SEA
Ural Mountains
Asiatic Russian Federation
Northern Dvina
Lake Onega
Lake Ladoga
Helsinki, FINLAND
Tallinn, ESTONIA
Riga, LATVIA
Vilnius, LITHUANIA
Minsk, BELARUS
Western Dvina
North European Plain
Moscow, RUSSIAN FEDERATION
Kiev, UKRAINE
Dnieper
Dniester
Volga
Don
Chisinau, MOLDOVA
Carpathian Mountains
CASPIAN SEA
SEA OF AZOV
Caucasus
Bucharest, ROMANIA
Sofia, BULGARIA
BLACK SEA
Danube
TURKEY
Balkan Mountains
Asian Turkey
AEGEAN SEA
Athens, GREECE
This way for Cyprus

Speech bubbles / captions:
It's plain to see.
I think I've lost a piece.
out of my way!
Almost there...
That gives me piece of mind.
I need a longer tape measurer.
Easy does it!
I'm puzzled.
I'm all at sea.
Are we missing a piece?
This is the life.
This place is a dive.
Good reef!
Don't leave me on the shelf!
What a shelf life!
Woohoo!
Hello
Watch my nose dive.
It's a slippery slope.
It's a current affair.

39
40

ZARRE BAZAAR

...a is one of the world's busiest marketplaces, home to ...ur billion people buying, selling, preparing, producing, and ...facturing everything that can possibly be needed in their daily ... Carpets and rugs, fresh food and cooked delicacies, televisions ...ars, ships and computers—all these and much more ...r sale somewhere in this bustling bazaar.

Russian Federation

Even without its European part, Siberia—as Asian Russia is known—would still be the biggest country in the world. It is sparsely occupied, since the winters are very harsh and the summers short.

Trans-Siberian railway

The 5,785-mile (9,310-km) Trans-Siberian railway runs from Moscow in the west across Siberia to Vladivostok in the east, with a journey time of eight days to travel from end to end.

Natural resources

Siberia is rich in timber and has huge oil, gas, and mineral reserves, although many are in remote parts of the country and difficult to access.

Siberian tiger

No more than 500 of these beautiful beasts—the largest tigers in the world—survive in the wilds of far eastern Siberia.

Chess

The national game of Russia, chess is regularly played in Siberia during the long winter nights.

Carpets

Turkish woven kilims, or carpets, are famous throughout the world for their intricate abstract designs.

...key

..., like Russia, crosses ...tinents of Asia and ... although most of it is ... Its Mediterranean coast ...many tourists and is an ...nt source of income.

APRICOTS

TURKISH DELIGHT

KEBABS

SPICED MEATBALLS

FIGS

Azerbaijan

Meaning "land of the flames" after the 8th-century Persians saw burning natural gas escaping from the ground, Azerbaijan exports much oil and natural gas to Europe.

...gion of the Caspian Sea is ...prized source of caviar— ...sive delicacy.

The Caucasus

The three small, mountainous, and largely agricultural states of the Caucasus lie squashed between the powerful neighboring states of Russia, Iran, and Turkey.

Georgia

Sheltered from cold north winds by the Caucasus mountains, Georgia is a major producer of grapes for wine.

Armenia

The world's oldest Christian nation, Armenia relies primarily on farming, notably sheep rearing, as its main industry.

Textiles

Georgia's significant silk and textile industry forms an important part of its economy.

The Near East

...Bordered by the eastern Mediterranean Sea, ...with the River Jordan running through it, ...this ancient region was the birthplace ...of some of the world's oldest ...civilizations and religions.

Syria

Cotton is one of the main cash crops grown in Syria, alongside fruit and vegetables.

Lebanon

The national symbol of Lebanon, cedar trees survive in a few protected woods and can live for more than 1,500 years.

Kibbe—a fried ball of lamb, cracked wheat, and onions—is the national dish of Lebanon.

Iran

Islamic spiritual leaders have governed the ancient country of Iran since 1979, making it one of the only two theocracies in the world.

Carpets

Iran is famous for its closely woven, intricately designed carpets and rugs that take many months to complete.

Architecture

Many old Iranian mosques are decorated in brightly colored tiles, with gold domes and tall minarets from which the faithful are called to prayer.

SHAH MOSQUE AT ISFAHAN

PERSIA—ANCIENT IRAN—WAS FAMOUS FOR ITS MINIATURE PAINTINGS.

Iraq

Lying across the fertile Tigris and Euphrates river valleys, Iraq is dominated by scorching desert in the south and west of the country, and mountains in its north and east.

Ancient Iraq

The ziggurat at Ur is one of many ancient buildings from the world's earliest and most advanced civilizations that flourished in Iraq more than 5,000 years ago.

Oil

Iraq has significantly vast natural gas reserves, as well as the third-largest oil reserves in the world.

The Gulf States

The south and west shores of the Gulf are occupied by a number of small Arab emirates, or kingdoms. All are awash in oil and gas and are using the money to develop other industries as well as tourism.

Oman

The seas off Oman teem with fish, including tuna, anchovies, sardines, and cuttlefish, and are now being exploited by local fishermen.

Yemen

It is thought that drinking coffee originated in Yemen, which still produces some of the world's finest coffee beans today.

Saudi Arabia

Oil has made Saudi Arabia fabulously rich, enabling it to develop new industries and build desalination plants—for turning seawater into useable freshwater.

Arabia

The Arabian peninsula mainly consists of a hot, dry desert that sits on top of the world's largest reserves of oil and natural gas, which have brought immense wealth to the region.

Israel

Israel was founded in 1948 as a homeland for Jews from around the world, but it is also home to many Palestinian Muslims and Christians.

Palestine

The River Jordan is the lowest river in the world. On its west bank, as well as in the Gaza Strip, Palestinians enjoy a limited home rule.

Jordan

The salt of the Dead Sea is collected and used in cooking and preserving food, while some people find the waters have healing properties.

Central Asia

The five "stans" or "lands" of Central Asia all became independent in 1991 after years of Russian rule. While Turkmenistan and Uzbekistan are largely flat and desertlike, Kyrgyzstan and Tajikistan are mountainous, and Kazakhstan consists of rolling steppes.

Kuwait

Kuwait's oil reserves, which are the fifth largest in the world, have fueled the country's prosperity.

Bahrain

The tiny island nation of Bahrain was once a major producer of pearls, although oil and gas have transformed the local economy.

Qatar

The flat, dry, desert peninsula of Qatar relies on its abundance of oil and gas, since oil production and refining form the basis of its economy.

United Arab Emirates

In 1971 seven separate emirates came together to form a single, federated country: the UAE. One of the emirates—Dubai—has built extraordinary fan-shaped developments in the sea to attract foreign tourists.

Speech bubbles:

Quick! There's a sale this way.

All this rushin'.

Take my picture!

Whose turn is it?

I'd better check.

Nice kitty!

From rugs to riches!

Fish eggs? Yuck!

More for me!

Let's get knitting.

This would make a good yarn.

Smooth as silk.

They're too high.

Don't whine.

Quick, these are a bargain.

Nice carpet!

I worked my magic.

Are you stringing me along?

They're packed like sardines.

How's your coffee?

The finest cup ever.

I'm naturally reserved.

This is immense!

He's barrels of fun.

Hooray!

I'm a big fan of the architecture.

Too much salt is bad for you.

No it's not.

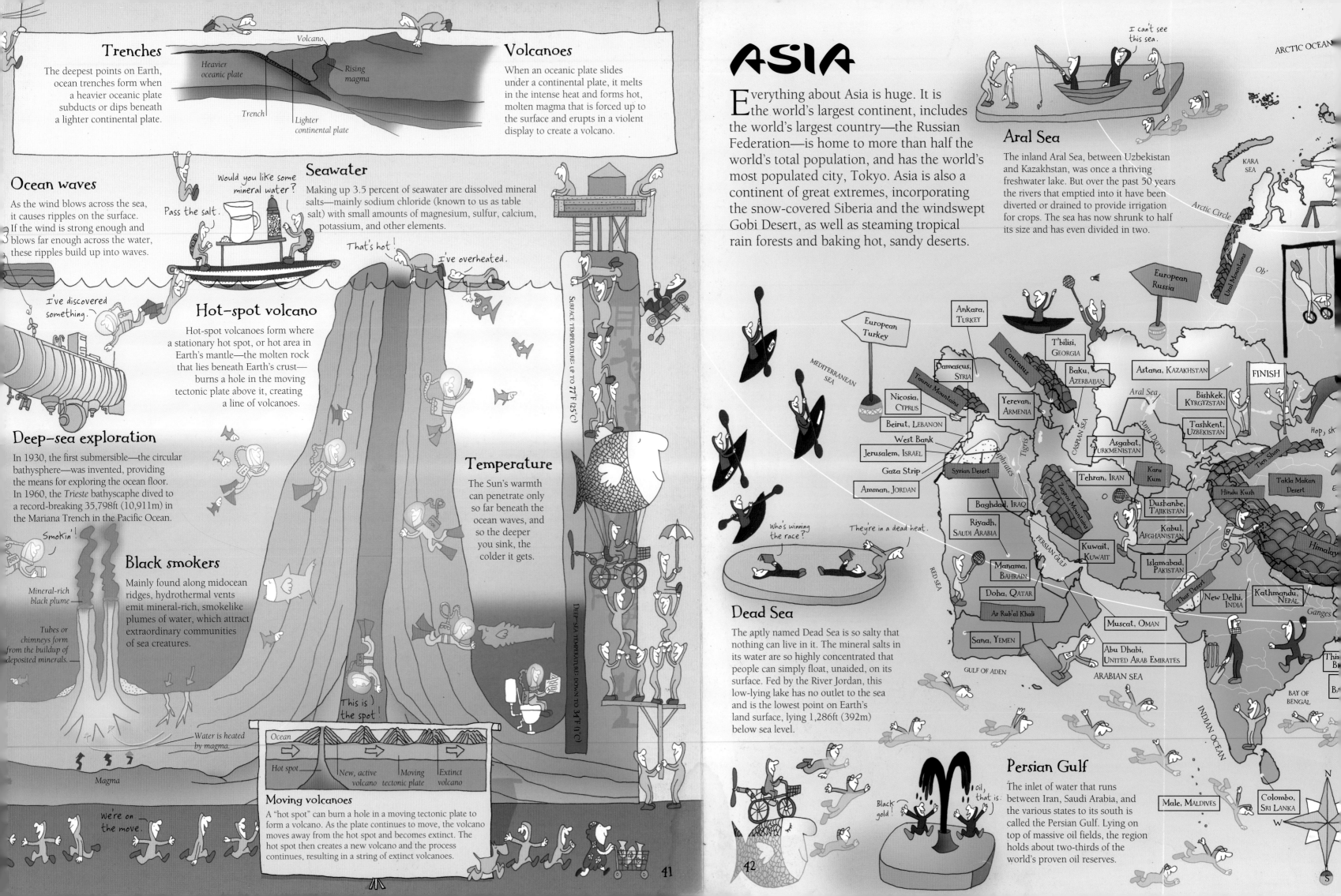

Trenches

The deepest points on Earth, ocean trenches form when a heavier oceanic plate subducts or dips beneath a lighter continental plate.

Volcano
Heavier oceanic plate
Rising magma
Trench
Lighter continental plate

Volcanoes

When an oceanic plate slides under a continental plate, it melts in the intense heat and forms hot, molten magma that is forced up to the surface and erupts in a violent display to create a volcano.

Ocean waves

As the wind blows across the sea, it causes ripples on the surface. If the wind is strong enough and blows far enough across the water, these ripples build up into waves.

Pass the salt.

Would you like some mineral water?

Seawater

Making up 3.5 percent of seawater are dissolved mineral salts—mainly sodium chloride (known to us as table salt) with small amounts of magnesium, sulfur, calcium, potassium, and other elements.

That's hot!

I've overheated.

I've discovered something.

Hot-spot volcano

Hot-spot volcanoes form where a stationary hot spot, or hot area in Earth's mantle—the molten rock that lies beneath Earth's crust—burns a hole in the moving tectonic plate above it, creating a line of volcanoes.

Surface temperature: up to 77°F (25°C)

Deep-sea exploration

In 1930, the first submersible—the circular bathysphere—was invented, providing the means for exploring the ocean floor. In 1960, the *Trieste* bathyscaphe dived to a record-breaking 35,798ft (10,911m) in the Mariana Trench in the Pacific Ocean.

Temperature

The Sun's warmth can penetrate only so far beneath the ocean waves, and so the deeper you sink, the colder it gets.

Smokin'!

Mineral-rich black plume

Black smokers

Mainly found along midocean ridges, hydrothermal vents emit mineral-rich, smokelike plumes of water, which attract extraordinary communities of sea creatures.

Tubes or chimneys form from the buildup of deposited minerals.

Deep-sea temperature: down to 34°F (1°C)

This is the spot!

Water is heated by magma.

Magma

We're on the move.

Moving volcanoes

A "hot spot" can burn a hole in a moving tectonic plate to form a volcano. As the plate continues to move, the volcano moves away from the hot spot and becomes extinct. The hot spot then creates a new volcano and the process continues, resulting in a string of extinct volcanoes.

Ocean
Hot spot
New, active volcano
Moving tectonic plate
Extinct volcano

ASIA

Everything about Asia is huge. It is the world's largest continent, includes the world's largest country—the Russian Federation—is home to more than half the world's total population, and has the world's most populated city, Tokyo. Asia is also a continent of great extremes, incorporating the snow-covered Siberia and the windswept Gobi Desert, as well as steaming tropical rain forests and baking hot, sandy deserts.

I can't see this sea.

Aral Sea

The inland Aral Sea, between Uzbekistan and Kazakhstan, was once a thriving freshwater lake. But over the past 50 years the rivers that emptied into it have been diverted or drained to provide irrigation for crops. The sea has now shrunk to half its size and has even divided in two.

ARCTIC OCEAN
KARA SEA
Arctic Circle
European Russia
Ural Mountains
Ob'

European Turkey

Ankara, TURKEY
T'bilisi, GEORGIA
Baku, AZERBAIJAN
Astana, KAZAKHSTAN
FINISH

MEDITERRANEAN SEA
Damascus, SYRIA
Caucasus
Taurus Mountains
Yerevan, ARMENIA
Aral Sea
Bishkek, KYRGYZSTAN

Nicosia, CYPRUS
CASPIAN SEA
Amu Darya
Tashkent, UZBEKISTAN

Beirut, LEBANON
Tehran, IRAN
Kara Kum
Tien Shan

West Bank
Tigris
Ashgabat, TURKMENISTAN
Takla Makan Desert

Jerusalem, ISRAEL
Euphrates
Zagros Mountains
Dushanbe, TAJIKISTAN
Hindu Kush

Gaza Strip
Syrian Desert
Kabul, AFGHANISTAN

Amman, JORDAN
Baghdad, IRAQ
Islamabad, PAKISTAN
Himalaya

Who's winning the race?

They're in a dead heat.

Riyadh, SAUDI ARABIA
PERSIAN GULF
Kuwait, KUWAIT

Manama, BAHRAIN
RED SEA
Thar Desert
New Delhi, INDIA
Kathmandu, NEPAL

Dead Sea

The aptly named Dead Sea is so salty that nothing can live in it. The mineral salts in its water are so highly concentrated that people can simply float, unaided, on its surface. Fed by the River Jordan, this low-lying lake has no outlet to the sea and is the lowest point on Earth's land surface, lying 1,286ft (392m) below sea level.

Doha, QATAR
Ar Rub'al Khali
Muscat, OMAN
Ganges

Sana, YEMEN
Abu Dhabi, UNITED ARAB EMIRATES

GULF OF ADEN
ARABIAN SEA
BAY OF BENGAL

Black gold!
Oil, that is.

Persian Gulf

The inlet of water that runs between Iran, Saudi Arabia, and the various states to its south is called the Persian Gulf. Lying on top of massive oil fields, the region holds about two-thirds of the world's proven oil reserves.

Male, MALDIVES
Colombo, SRI LANKA
INDIAN OCEAN

Uzbekistan

Uzbekistan is a major producer of cotton, and also has one of the world's largest gold mines, as well as vast reserves of natural gas and oil.

It's a top pick!

Kazakhstan

The first Kazakhs were nomads who traveled around on horses. Horse-racing remains popular today, while kumis—fermented mare's milk—is the national drink. Cheers!

Kyrgyzstan

Mountainous Kyrgyzstan has a wealth of exploitable natural resources: the perfect landscape for hydroelectric power stations, and vast reserves of mercury and gold, which it exports.

Did someone break a thermometer?

Tajikistan

Its plentiful supplies of uranium, used in nuclear power generation, are the mainstay of Tajikistan's economy.

Atomic!

[...]istan

[...] the Turkmen" [...]amous for its [...]tional emblem.

Hold your horses.

Are we packed yet?

Central Southern Asia

The Muslim countries of Afghanistan and Pakistan lie sandwiched between India, Iran, and central Asia. Both countries are home to many different peoples speaking many different languages.

This is industrial-strength cotton.

Pakistan

An important cotton-producer, Pakistan has developed a large textile industry around this.

By bus

The brightly decorated buses, often lit by holiday lights, are the most colorful way to travel around Pakistan.

Afghanistan

The different groups of peoples that live in Afghanistan traditionally have their own distinguishable hats.

...arakul sheep
[...] farmers breed the [...]—one of the oldest [...] sheep breeds—for [...]inctive curly fleece.

Baa!

Spinning cotton

The chakra, or spinning wheel, became a symbol for Indian independence through inspirational leader Mahatma Gandhi.

I like my independence.

This is wheelie cool.

Indian subcontinent

With more than one-fifth of the world's population, the Indian subcontinent is home to many different ethnic groups and religions, epitomized by the symbolic Lotus Temple in New Delhi, in which followers of all religions are invited to worship.

It's a wrap.

Nepal

Native Nepalese known as Sherpas serve as guides for the many mountaineers who come to climb Everest and other Himalayan mountains.

Does this strike a cord?

Bollywood

A fusing of "Bombay" (as Mumbai used to be known) with "Hollywood," the term "Bollywood" refers to a particular style of Indian film, popular among Indians living throughout the world.

[...]s only Buddhist kingdom, [...]s high up in the Himalayas. [...] are tended for their meat, and tails.

TAJ MAHAL—BUILT BY MOGUL EMPEROR SHAH JAHAN TO COMMEMORATE HIS WIFE MUMTAZ, WHO DIED IN 1631

Maldives

Coconuts are an important harvest in the Maldives, where tuna fishing and tourism are also major industries.

Incoming!

[...]gladesh is ideal for [...] a tough, fibrous plant [...] make rope, sacking, [...]cking.

Sri Lanka

Sri Lanka is the world's second largest producer of tea, which is grown in the country's humid, hilly interior.

Tea for two.

East Asia

The ancient country of China is today the world's most populated nation, with the fastest-growing economy. To its north is Mongolia—a landlocked country that is rich in mineral resources.

Did they consider building a fence?

The Great Wall of China

First constructed around 200BC and then much enlarged and lengthened, the world's longest structure—at almost 4,000 miles (6,400km) long—snakes across China.

This is great!

Panda

Found only in China, there are only about 1,600 of the lovable giant pandas surviving in the wild today.

Chop, chop.

I'll pander to your every need.

Chinese food

Star anise and other spices are used to flavor Chinese food, which is eaten out of small bowls using two wooden sticks known as chopsticks.

Taiwan

The offshore island of Taiwan relies on its exports of electronic and electrical goods, which have made it one of the world's most successful industrial economies.

Horse skills

Riding horses for pleasure, racing, hunting, and sport, many Mongols are highly skilled horse riders.

Don't be a neigh sayer.

Get off your high horse!

Mongolia

Mongolia is one of the most sparsely populated countries in the world, with many of its nomadic people living in traditional felt yurts or tents.

Maritime Southeast Asia

The tropical island nations off the southeast coast of Asia include Indonesia—the largest archipelago in the world with more than 18,000 islands.

Let's drum up support

I play the oil drum.

Brunei

Following the discovery of oil underneath this tiny kingdom, Brunei is today one of the world's richest countries.

Some cars for your oil?

East Timor

The waters off this tiny nation contain one of the richest oil fields in the world outside the Middle East.

Philippines

The Philippines are the second-largest producer of coconuts in the world. They are used to make many useful products.

BASKETS MADE FROM PALM LEAVES

MATS MADE FROM THE COCONUT'S OUTER HUSK

COCONUT MEAT AND MILK IS USED IN COOKING

Indonesia

Gamelans—tuned percussion orchestras—accompany dancers in ritual and religious ceremonies.

Myanmar (Burma)

The deep-red rubies mined in Burma are considered to be the best in the world.

You're the best.

Singapore

The island nation of Singapore is the world's busiest port, handling ships from China, Japan, the Middle East, and Europe.

Top stuff!

Malaysia

Malaysia is one of the world's top producers of palm oil, from coconuts, used in cooking and to make soap.

Thailand

Many of the markets in Bangkok, the Thai capital, are on the water, with traders selling their goods from floating sampans.

Southeast Asia

Seven nations are crowded onto the southeast Asian peninsula. Their peoples are a mix of Hindus, Buddhists, and Muslims with a rich mixture of beliefs and cultures.

Vietnam

Much of Vietnam's farmland is underwater during the year, since the country is a leading producer and exporter of rice.

What a pretty paddy.

Cambodia

Once the center of the Khmer Empire, Cambodia's jungles reveal such structures as the vast 12th-century temple of Angkor Wat.

Angkor what?

Laos

Meaning "Mother of rivers," the Mekong in Laos is a rich source of fish, irrigation water for the paddy fields, and serves as the country's main watery highway.

North Korea

The root of the ginseng plant, grown in both North and South Korea, is believed to nurture good health and energy.

Such definition!

South Korea

One-third of the world's new ships come from South Korean shipyards, which work at an impressive rate to complete a new ship once every four working days!

It's ship shape.

Traditional Japanese dress includes kimonos and geta, or wooden clogs.

Kimono over sometime.

Japan

The Japanese excel at making electronic goods, leading the world in computers and consumer goods.

Japan and Korea

Both South Korea and the island nation of Japan have highly developed industrial economies, producing everything from ships and cars to computers and high-definition televisions.

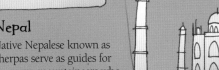

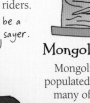

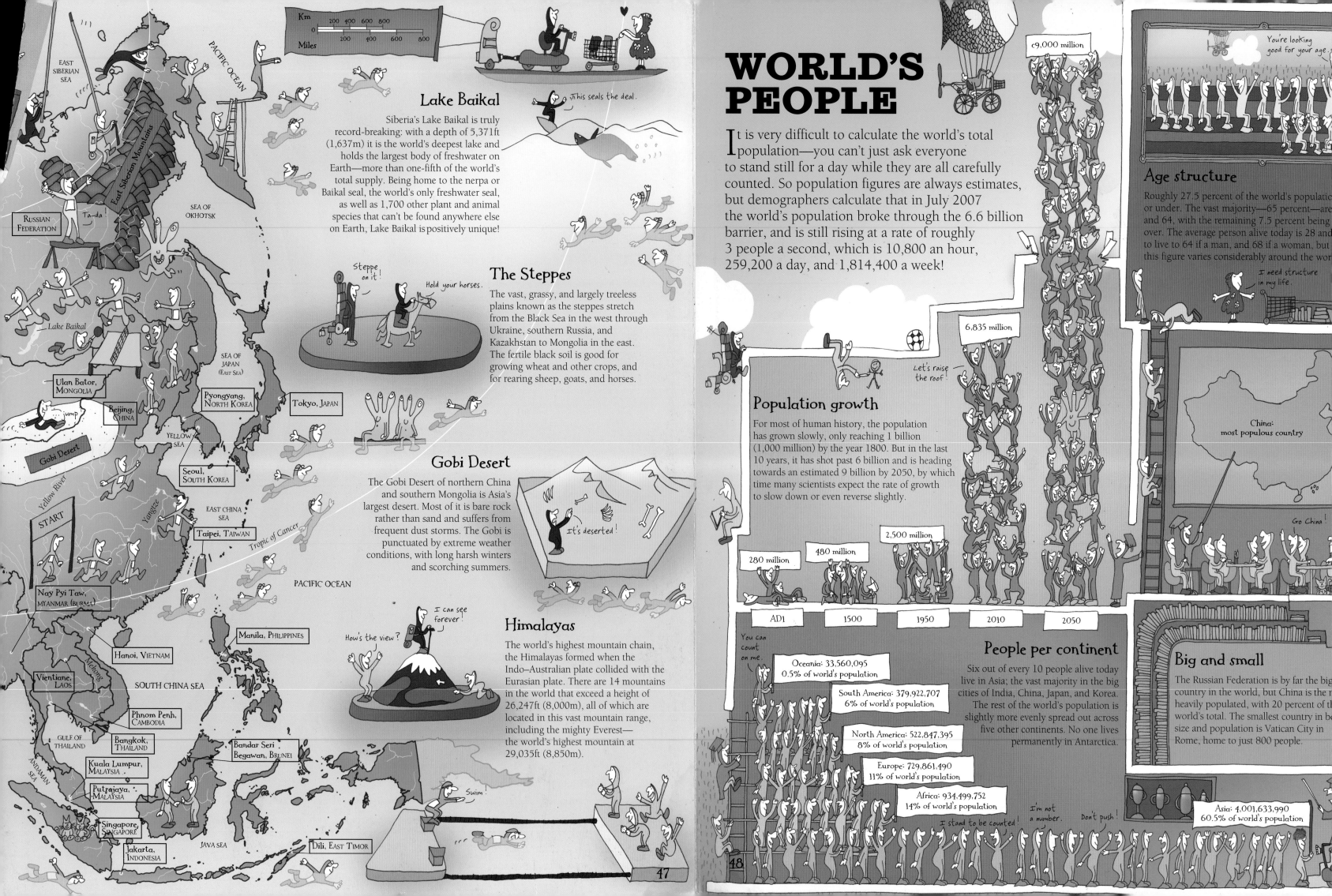

Lake Baikal

Siberia's Lake Baikal is truly record-breaking: with a depth of 5,371ft (1,637m) it is the world's deepest lake and holds the largest body of freshwater on Earth—more than one-fifth of the world's total supply. Being home to the nerpa or Baikal seal, the world's only freshwater seal, as well as 1,700 other plant and animal species that can't be found anywhere else on Earth, Lake Baikal is positively unique!

The Steppes

The vast, grassy, and largely treeless plains known as the steppes stretch from the Black Sea in the west through Ukraine, southern Russia, and Kazakhstan to Mongolia in the east. The fertile black soil is good for growing wheat and other crops, and for rearing sheep, goats, and horses.

Gobi Desert

The Gobi Desert of northern China and southern Mongolia is Asia's largest desert. Most of it is bare rock rather than sand and suffers from frequent dust storms. The Gobi is punctuated by extreme weather conditions, with long harsh winters and scorching summers.

Himalayas

The world's highest mountain chain, the Himalayas formed when the Indo–Australian plate collided with the Eurasian plate. There are 14 mountains in the world that exceed a height of 26,247ft (8,000m), all of which are located in this vast mountain range, including the mighty Everest— the world's highest mountain at 29,035ft (8,850m).

WORLD'S PEOPLE

It is very difficult to calculate the world's total population—you can't just ask everyone to stand still for a day while they are all carefully counted. So population figures are always estimates, but demographers calculate that in July 2007 the world's population broke through the 6.6 billion barrier, and is still rising at a rate of roughly 3 people a second, which is 10,800 an hour, 259,200 a day, and 1,814,400 a week!

Age structure

Roughly 27.5 percent of the world's population or under. The vast majority—65 percent—are and 64, with the remaining 7.5 percent being over. The average person alive today is 28 to live to 64 if a man, and 68 if a woman, but this figure varies considerably around the wor

Population growth

For most of human history, the population has grown slowly, only reaching 1 billion (1,000 million) by the year 1800. But in the last 10 years, it has shot past 6 billion and is heading towards an estimated 9 billion by 2050, by which time many scientists expect the rate of growth to slow down or even reverse slightly.

c9,000 million

6,835 million

2,500 million

480 million

280 million

| AD1 | 1500 | 1950 | 2010 | 2050 |

People per continent

Six out of every 10 people alive today live in Asia; the vast majority in the big cities of India, China, Japan, and Korea. The rest of the world's population is slightly more evenly spread out across five other continents. No one lives permanently in Antarctica.

Oceania: 33,560,095
0.5% of world's population

South America: 379,922,707
6% of world's population

North America: 522,847,395
8% of world's population

Europe: 729,861,490
11% of world's population

Africa: 934,499,752
14% of world's population

Asia: 4,001,633,990
60.5% of world's population

Big and small

The Russian Federation is by far the big country in the world, but China is the r heavily populated, with 20 percent of th world's total. The smallest country in b size and population is Vatican City in Rome, home to just 800 people.

EACH BARBECUE

Around 33 million people live in Oceania, with the vast majority of them residing in the towns and cities of coastal Australia and New Zealand. Pacific islanders live on three main groups of islands—Micronesia, Melanesia, Polynesia—and share similar languages and customs, although the vast distances between the islands make communication difficult and travel expensive.

Australia

A huge, mostly flat country, Australia largely consists of a vast, hot, inland desert, which is why nine-tenths of Australians live by the cooler coast. The Aborigines, Australia's first inhabitants, arrived from Asia 40,000 years ago. Europeans arrived in 1788 and now make up the overwhelming majority of the population.

Canberra

Unable to choose between Sydney and Melbourne as Australia's capital city, it was decided to build a new capital—Canberra—midway between the two.

Sydney

The largest and oldest city in Australia, Sydney lies around a large, sheltered harbor, with its iconic Opera House and world-famous Harbour Bridge.

Uluru / Ayers Rock

A massive outcrop of red sandstone carved by the wind and sandstorms, Uluru is considered a sacred site by the local Aborigines.

Aborigine culture

The Aborigines developed a sophisticated musical culture, based on a long bamboo or hardwood pipe that makes a deep, echoing sound—the didgeridoo.

Wildlife

Unique to the continent are kangaroos, koalas, black swans, plus the world's only egg-laying mammals—platypuses and echidnas.

World's largest butterfly

Found only in New Guinea, the Queen Alexandra's birdwing butterfly has a wingspan of up to 1ft (30cm).

Languages

More than 750 different languages are spoken in Papua New Guinea—more than in any other country in the world. English is the country's official language.

Flying doctors

Some farms and small settlements in Australia's Outback are so remote that the only way doctors can reach their patients in time is by airplane.

Great Barrier Reef

The breathtakingly beautiful Great Barrier Reef lies just under the waves—an ideal place for divers to see the spectacular fish and corals of the reef.

Mining

The gold mines of Papua New Guinea are among the largest in the world. Copper, silver, nickel, and cobalt are also mined.

Papua New Guinea

A mostly mountainous country covered with tropical rain forest, Papua New Guinea occupies the eastern end of New Guinea—the world's third largest island—and includes 600 other small islands, spread out across the Pacific.

Surfing

Australians are sports-crazy, surfing the great waves that pound their shores, sailing the seas, as well as playing Australian Rules football, rugby, cricket, and tennis.

Grapes

Southeast Australia's warm, dry climate is ideal for growing grapes and other fruit. Its successful vineyards have made it the fourth largest wine exporter in the world.

Mining

Australia has one of the world's most important mining industries, with vast reserves of coal, iron ore, gold, copper, and bauxite—used to make aluminum.

First languages spoken

There are about 6,900 languages spoken in the world today, some spoken by millions of people, others by less than 1,000, and many people speak more than one language.

ESTIMATES OF FIRST LANGUAGES

MANDARIN CHINESE spoken by 873 million
SPANISH spoken by 322 million
ENGLISH spoken by 309 million
PORTUGUESE spoken by 230 million
ARABIC spoken by 206 million

World religions

The major world religions were all founded around 1,400 years ago, but new religions are still forming today. About 16 percent of the world's population has no religion.

Buddhist 6% Jewish 0.2% Christian 33%

Muslim 21% Hindu 14% Sikh 0.4%

Largest urban areas

It is very difficult to estimate the population of a city, as people come and go every day, and the boundary of what is in and outside the city is not always clear—it will often sprawl beyond its political boundary. Therefore, the population figures below are estimates for each entire built-up area.

- Tokyo 32,450,000
- Seoul 20,550,000
- Mexico City 20,450,000
- New York 19,750,000
- Mumbai 19,200,000
- Jakarta 18,900,000
- Sao Paolo 18,850,000
- Delhi 18,600,000
- Osaka 17,375,000
- Shanghai 16,650,000

Political systems

Every country has its own political system but they can be grouped into roughly four main types: a republic like France where people vote for their head of state and government; a monarchy like Britain where the head of state is hereditary; a dictatorship like Myanmar (Burma) where a strong man or the army is in control; and a theocracy like Iran where priests rule according to religious laws.

Republic   Monarchy   Dictatorship   Theocracy

World wealth

People's different jobs and occupations can all be grouped together in three main sectors: agriculture, industry, and services (such as banking or tourism). However, there is a huge difference between the number of people working in each sector and the proportion of the world's wealth that each sector produces.

- 41% of world's labour force — 4% of world's wealth — Agriculture
- 20% of world's labour force — 32% of world's wealth — Industry
- 39% of world's labour force — 64% of world's wealth — Services

Town and country

Throughout human history, more people have lived in the countryside than in the towns. At some point in 2008, that balance shifted, and now more people live in the world's ever-growing towns than in the country.

OCEANIA

This enormous watery region consists of the island continent of Australia, the large island groups of New Zealand and Papua New Guinea, and 11 independent island nations and other territories strung out across the vast distances of the southern Pacific Ocean.

The Outback

The center of Australia is known as the Outback and is one of the hottest, driest areas on Earth. Most of the Outback consists of sandy or stony desert, dotted with mountain ranges and a few rocky outcrops, including Uluru, or Ayers Rock, the world's largest free-standing rock.

Saipan, NORTHERN MARIANA ISLANDS (to USA)
Hagatna, GUAM (to USA)
Palikir, MICRONESIA
Majuro Atoll, MARSHALL ISLANDS
Bairiki, KIRIBATI
NAURU
Melekeok, PALAU
Honiara, SOLOMON ISLANDS
Port Moresby, PAPUA NEW GUINEA
Port–Vila, VANUATU
Nouméa, NEW CALEDONIA (to France)
CORAL SEA ISLANDS (to Australia)
Canberra, AUSTRALIA
Wellington, NEW ZEALAND

ARAFURA SEA
TIMOR SEA
CORAL SEA
INDIAN OCEAN
Cape York Peninsula
Arnhem Land
Kimberley Plateau
Northern Territory
Great Sandy Desert
Tanami Desert
Simpson Desert
Gibson Desert
Great Victoria Desert
Western Australia
South Australia
Queensland
Great Barrier Reef
Great Dividing Range
Lake Eyre
Lake Torrens
Flinders Ranges
New South Wales
Darling
Murray
Nullarbor Plain
Great Australian Bight
BASS STRAIT
TASMANIA
TASMAN SEA
Equator

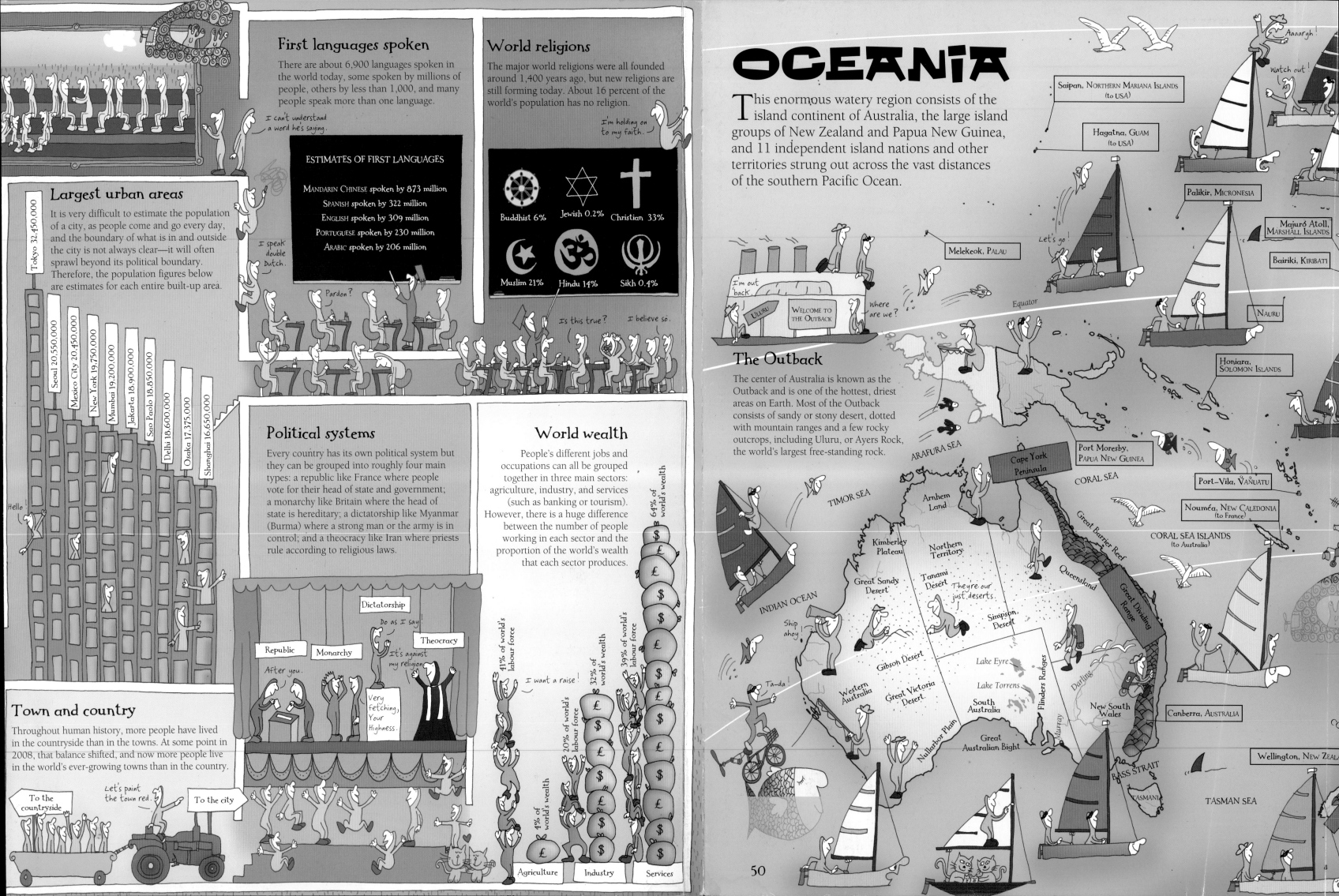

Micronesia (partial, left edge)
...shall Islands, Nauru, Palau, and the Federated States ...nesia, as well as the U.S. territories of Guam, Wake ...nd the Northern Mariana Islands, make up the region ...ollectively as Micronesia in the northwest Pacific.

Palau
With an abundance of palm trees, Palau's islanders harvest coconuts for their copra—the dried kernel or nut that is made into coconut oil.

Micronesia
Coral atolls and an array of shipwrecks from World War II attract many scuba-diving tourists to the Federated States of Micronesia..

Nauru
...rld's smallest republic, Nauru has ...ndscape following the exhaustive ...of its vast reserves of phosphate.

Marshall Islands
Like many others in the Pacific, the inhabitants of the Marshall Islands fear that rising sea levels may engulf their low-lying island nation.

Guam
A major U.S. military base covers one-third of this tropical island, which also entices many tourists.

Solomon Islands
The heavily wooded Solomon Islands introduced a sustainable forest-harvesting policy in 1998 to prevent illegal logging and deforestation.

(Melanesia) (partial, left edge)
...sian islands of the southwest Pacific are mostly ...origin and consist of Fiji, the Solomon Islands, ...d French-owned New Caledonia.

Vanuatu
Once known as the New Hebrides until its independence in 1980, Vanuatu today relies on its exports of cocoa and coconut products.

Fiji
The main crop grown on Fiji is sugar cane, which is exported along with copra and gold.

(Polynesia) (partial, left edge)
...g Polynesian islands include Kiribati, Samoa, Tonga, and ...New Zealand–administered Cook Islands, Niue, and Tokelau; ...nesia and Wallis and Futuna; the British-owned Pitcairn ...distant Easter Island, administered by Chile.

Hawaii
Lying to the north of Polynesia, Hawaii, formed by the peaks of the world's tallest volcanoes, is the 50th state of the U.S. and a major tourist destination.

Kiribati
Like many Pacific nations, Kiribati's farmers harvest the coconut and use every part of it: copra for oil, and coir fibers for ropes, mats, and brushes.

Tuvalu
In 1998 Tuvalu sold its ".tv" domain name for use on the Internet by television-related Web sites, bringing in millions of dollars.

Tonga
Uniquely among the Pacific islands, Tonga was never fully colonized and kept its own monarchy.

Samoa
Forestry and agriculture provide the main exports for this island nation, while tourism boosts the local income.

Whale watching
The seas around New Zealand are full of marine mammals, including dolphins, porpoises, and whales, which can often be glimpsed close to the shore.

The kiwi
The national emblem of New Zealand, the flightless kiwi bird sleeps during the day and is closely related to the ostrich and the emu.

Maori
The original Polynesian inhabitants of New Zealand preserve many of their customs, including greeting each other with a hongi (rubbing noses).

Rugby
The All Blacks—the national rugby team—won the first Rugby World Cup in 1987 and continue to be one of the most successful teams in the world.

Auckland
Known as the City of Sails, Auckland is famous for its huge number of yachts and other boats, and is home to more than a third of New Zealand's population.

Bungee jumping
Many tourists traveling through New Zealand will stop off for an attempt at bungee jumping, which was invented here.

Geysers
New Zealand lies on a fault between two moving tectonic plates, resulting in its North Island being dotted with grand geysers, hot mud springs, and active volcanoes.

Sheep
Wool and lamb are major exports for New Zealand, where there are 10 sheep to every person.

New Zealand
Consisting of two large and many smaller islands, New Zealand lies some 992 miles (1,600km) southeast of Australia. Its South Island is mountainous, while North Island, where most people live, is more volcanic.

Cook Islands
Fishing for giant clams and pearls is a major source of income for the Cook Islands, as is tourism, while nearby Niue and Tokelau largely rely on the sale of postage stamps and coins.

French Polynesia
Nearly three-quarters of French Polynesia's population live on the island of Tahiti, although the territory includes some 130 other islands.

Pitcairn Islands
The remote Pitcairn Islands are home to descendants of mutineers from the HMS *Bounty*, who landed on the islands in 1790.

Easter Island
Discovered by Europeans on Easter Sunday, Easter Island boasts a series of impressive 400–900-year-old stone statues.

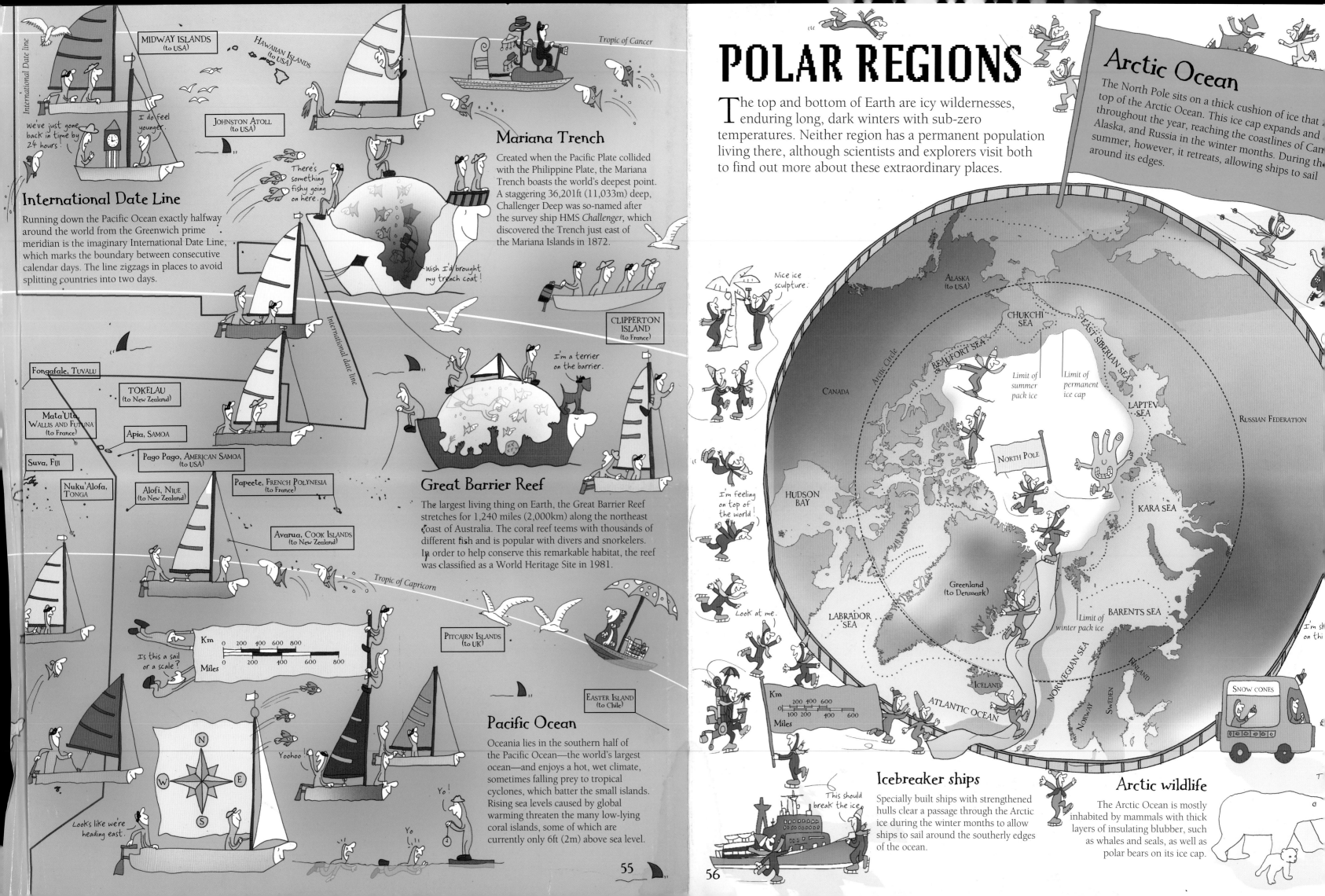

International Date Line

Running down the Pacific Ocean exactly halfway around the world from the Greenwich prime meridian is the imaginary International Date Line, which marks the boundary between consecutive calendar days. The line zigzags in places to avoid splitting countries into two days.

Mariana Trench

Created when the Pacific Plate collided with the Philippine Plate, the Mariana Trench boasts the world's deepest point. A staggering 36,201ft (11,033m) deep, Challenger Deep was so-named after the survey ship HMS *Challenger*, which discovered the Trench just east of the Mariana Islands in 1872.

Great Barrier Reef

The largest living thing on Earth, the Great Barrier Reef stretches for 1,240 miles (2,000km) along the northeast coast of Australia. The coral reef teems with thousands of different fish and is popular with divers and snorkelers. In order to help conserve this remarkable habitat, the reef was classified as a World Heritage Site in 1981.

Pacific Ocean

Oceania lies in the southern half of the Pacific Ocean—the world's largest ocean—and enjoys a hot, wet climate, sometimes falling prey to tropical cyclones, which batter the small islands. Rising sea levels caused by global warming threaten the many low-lying coral islands, some of which are currently only 6ft (2m) above sea level.

MIDWAY ISLANDS (to USA)

HAWAIIAN ISLANDS (to USA)

Tropic of Cancer

We've just gone back in time by 24 hours!

I do feel younger.

JOHNSTON ATOLL (to USA)

There's something fishy going on here.

Wish I'd brought my trench coat!

CLIPPERTON ISLAND (to France)

I'm a terrier on the barrier.

Fongafale, TUVALU

TOKELAU (to New Zealand)

Mata'Utu, WALLIS AND FUTUNA (to France)

Apia, SAMOA

Suva, FIJI

Pago Pago, AMERICAN SAMOA (to USA)

Nuku'Alofa, TONGA

Alofi, NIUE (to New Zealand)

Papeete, FRENCH POLYNESIA (to France)

Avarua, COOK ISLANDS (to New Zealand)

Tropic of Capricorn

PITCAIRN ISLANDS (to UK)

Km 0 200 400 600 800
Miles 0 200 400 600 800

Is this a sail or a scale?

EASTER ISLAND (to Chile)

Yoohoo!

Yo!

Yo

Looks like we're heading east.

N W E S

55

POLAR REGIONS

The top and bottom of Earth are icy wildernesses, enduring long, dark winters with sub-zero temperatures. Neither region has a permanent population living there, although scientists and explorers visit both to find out more about these extraordinary places.

Arctic Ocean

The North Pole sits on a thick cushion of ice that [...] top of the Arctic Ocean. This ice cap expands and [...] throughout the year, reaching the coastlines of Can[...] Alaska, and Russia in the winter months. During the summer, however, it retreats, allowing ships to sail around its edges.

Nice ice sculpture.

ALASKA (to USA)

CHUKCHI SEA

EAST SIBERIAN SEA

Arctic Circle

BEAUFORT SEA

Limit of summer pack ice

Limit of permanent ice cap

LAPTEV SEA

CANADA

RUSSIAN FEDERATION

I'm feeling on top of the world!

NORTH POLE

KARA SEA

HUDSON BAY

Look at me.

Greenland (to Denmark)

BARENTS SEA

LABRADOR SEA

Limit of winter pack ice

NORWEGIAN SEA

FINLAND

I'm sk[...] on thi[...]

Km 200 400 600 / 100 200 400 600
Miles

ICELAND

ATLANTIC OCEAN

NORWAY

SWEDEN

SNOW CONES

This should break the ice.

Icebreaker ships

Specially built ships with strengthened hulls clear a passage through the Arctic ice during the winter months to allow ships to sail around the southerly edges of the ocean.

Arctic wildlife

The Arctic Ocean is mostly inhabited by mammals with thick layers of insulating blubber, such as whales and seals, as well as polar bears on its ice cap.

56

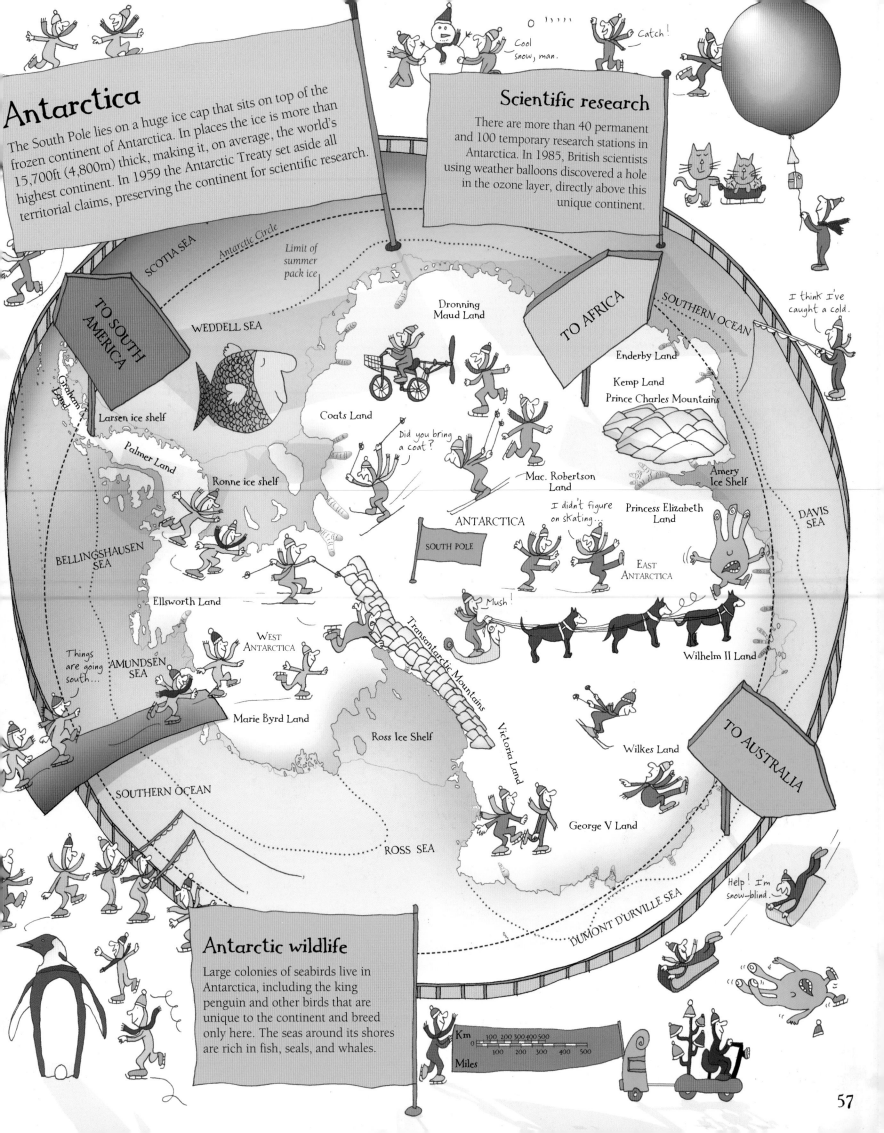

Antarctica

The South Pole lies on a huge ice cap that sits on top of the frozen continent of Antarctica. In places the ice is more than 15,700ft (4,800m) thick, making it, on average, the world's highest continent. In 1959 the Antarctic Treaty set aside all territorial claims, preserving the continent for scientific research.

Scientific research

There are more than 40 permanent and 100 temporary research stations in Antarctica. In 1985, British scientists using weather balloons discovered a hole in the ozone layer, directly above this unique continent.

Antarctic wildlife

Large colonies of seabirds live in Antarctica, including the king penguin and other birds that are unique to the continent and breed only here. The seas around its shores are rich in fish, seals, and whales.

COMPARATIVELY SPEAKING

Everyone likes compiling lists—their top 10 favorite books or CDs, or their top five places to visit. Geographers do it, too, compiling lists of the highest and longest, biggest and deepest natural features in the world.

Mountains

All 14 of the mighty mountains that are more than 26,256ft (8,000m) high are in the Himalayas, and all 109 mountains more than 23,630ft (7,200m) are in the mountain ranges of central Asia. Therefore, below is a comparison of the highest mountain of each continent.

Waterfalls

The height of a waterfall is measured by its vertical drop from top to bottom, although this fall can be broken by rocky outcrops on its way down. This causes disputes when comparing the heights, but every geographer agrees that Angel Falls in Venezuela is the world's highest waterfall.

Mt. Everest, Asia 29,035ft (8,850m)

Kilimanjaro, Africa 19,340ft (5,895m)

Vinson Massif, Antarctica 16,072ft (4,897m)

Aconcagua, South America 22,841ft (6,962m)

Mt. Wilhelm, Oceania 14,794ft (4,509m)

Mt. Elbrus, Europe 18,510ft (5,642m)

Mt. McKinley, North America 20,322ft (6,194m)

Angel, South America 3,212ft (979m)

Tugela, Africa 3,110ft (947m)

Utigard, Europe 2,625ft (800m)

Mongefossen, Europe 2,540ft (774m)

Mutarazi Falls, Africa 2,501ft (762m)

Land versus water

The land that we live on accounts for less than one-third of the world's surface; more than two-thirds are the watery habitats of oceans, seas, and lakes. And if sea levels continue to rise with global warming, this ratio will continue to increase.

Land 29.2% of Earth's surface

Oceans and seas 70.8% of Earth's surface

Continents

The seven continents that make up Earth's land area dramatically vary in size, from hefty Asia down to tiny Oceania.

North America 16% of Earth's land area

South America 12% of Earth's land area

Antarctica 9% of Earth's land area

Europe 7% of Earth's land area

Oceania 6% of Earth's land area

Asia 29% of Earth's land area

Africa 21% of Earth's land area

Lakes

It is rather confusing that the world's largest lake is called a sea, but the Caspian Sea is, by any definition, a lake, since it is completely surrounded by land.

Lake Superior, North America 32,151 sq miles (83,270 sq km)

Lake Huron, North America 23,000 sq miles (59,570 sq km)

Caspian Sea, Asia 143,243 sq miles (371,000 sq km)

Lake Victoria, Africa 26,828 sq miles (69,500 sq km)

Lake Michigan, North America 22,300 sq miles (57,750 sq km)

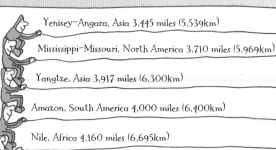

Yenisey–Angara, Asia 3,445 miles (5,539km)

Mississippi–Missouri, North America 3,710 miles (5,969km)

Yangtze, Asia 3,917 miles (6,300km)

Amazon, South America 4,000 miles (6,400km)

Nile, Africa 4,160 miles (6,695km)

Rivers

There is much debate about which river is really the longest—the Nile or the Amazon—due to irritating uncertainties about which tributary is the river's main source, and which direction the river takes through its delta to the sea. The Nile usually wins, but only barely!

GLOSSARY

Archipelago
A large group of islands.

Asteroid
A small, rocky planet orbiting the Sun.

Atmosphere
The thin layer of gases that surround Earth.

Climate
The typical weather recorded in a place over a period of 30 years or more.

Comet
An icy, rocky lump surrounded by a halo of gas and dust that orbits the Sun.

Communism
A system of government in which the state owns and controls everything on behalf of the people.

Continental plate
A tectonic plate that carries a continent.

Continental shelf
The gently sloping part of the ocean floor nearest to the shore.

Continental slope
The steep slope that leads from the continental shelf down to the continental rise and the seafloor.

Coral reef
An underwater structure formed by the accumulation of millions of coral polyp skeletons.

Crust
The hard outer shell of Earth.

Current
A mass of water flowing just below the surface of the ocean.

Delta
A fan-shaped, low-lying area of deposits at the mouth or end of a river.

Dictatorship
A form of government that has absolute control over a country, headed by a single individual, the army, or by a single political party.

Earthquake
A shaking of the ground caused by sudden movements in Earth's crust.

Eclipse
The total or partial covering of one heavenly body by another. A solar eclipse occurs when the Moon passes between the Sun and Earth; a lunar eclipse occurs when Earth passes between the Sun and Moon.

Equator
An imaginary line, midway between the two Poles, that divides the world into two equal halves, or hemispheres.

Fault
A crack or fracture in Earth's rocks caused by moving tectonic plates.

Geyser
A hot spring that throws up jets of boiling water and steam through a hole in Earth's crust.

Glacier
A moving river of ice.

Greenwich Prime Meridian
The line of 0° longitude, passing through Greenwich in London, from which the 24 time zones of the world are set.

Hemisphere
The northern or southern half of the world.

International Date Line
An imaginary line running down the length of the Pacific Ocean. When you cross it from west to east, you move the date on the calendar back one day to allow for the effect of the rotation of Earth around the Sun.

Landlocked
A country that has no access to the sea.

Latitude
The imaginary lines drawn parallel to the Equator that tell us how far north or south we are.

Lava
Magma that has emerged onto Earth's surface.

Longitude
The imaginary lines drawn around Earth from Pole to Pole that tell us how far east or west we are.

Magma
Hot, molten rock—created by the partial melting of Earth's crust and mantle—that emerges onto Earth's surface through a volcano.

Mantle
The soft interior of Earth that consists of solid rock and liquid magma and lies between Earth's core and its crust.

Monarchy
A kingdom or country whose head of state is a king or queen.

North Pole
The northern end of the axis around which Earth rotates.

Ocean
A vast, open expanse of seawater.

Ocean-basin floor
The deep part of the ocean beyond the continental shelf.

Ocean floor
All Earth's surface that is covered by water.

Oceanic plate
A tectonic plate that lies beneath an ocean.

Oceanic trench
A long, deep dip in the ocean floor.

Peninsula
A narrow strip of land projecting out into a sea or lake.

Planet
A celestial body that revolves around a star, from which it receives light; Earth is a planet that revolves around a star we call the Sun.

Republic
A country in which the people elect their head of state and government to rule them.

River basin
A dip or depression in Earth's surface that is drained by one river and its tributaries.

South Pole
The southern end of the axis around which Earth rotates.

Steppe
A grassy, largely treeless plain.

Tectonic plate
A plate that forms part of Earth's lithosphere – the rigid crust and upper mantle – and floats on the liquid mantle below.

Theocracy
A country that is ruled by religious leaders and religious laws.

Tornado
A small but intense spiraling windstorm formed beneath thunderclouds with wind speeds up to 250mph (400kph).

Tributary
A small river that joins a larger one.

Tropics
The area on either side of the Equator in which the midday Sun is generally overhead. The Tropic of Cancer is the line of latitude to the north of the tropics, the Tropic of Capricorn the line of latitude to the south.

Tsunami
A huge ocean wave set off by an underwater earthquake at sea.

Volcano
A gap in Earth's crust through which magma escapes.

Weather
A region's daily changes in factors such as wind, rainfall, and temperature.

INDEX

A

Abu Dhabi 42
Abuja 26
Accra 26
Addis Ababa 26
Afghanistan 42, 45
Africa 26–31, 48, 58
Albania 34, 38
Algeria 26, 27
Algiers 26
Alofi 55
Alps 34, 37
Amazon rain forest 18, 19
Amazon River 18, 58
American Samoa 55
Amman 42
Amsterdam 34
Andes 18, 20, 23
Andorra 34, 36
Andorra la Vella 34
Angel Falls 18, 58
Angola 30, 31
Ankara 42
Antananarivo 31
Antarctica 57, 58
Apia 55
Arabia 44
Aral Sea 42
Arctic Ocean 56
Argentina 20, 23
Armenia 43
Ashgabat 42
Asia 42–47, 48, 58
Asmara 26
Astana 42
Asunción 20, 23
Atacama Desert 20, 23
Athens 39
atmosphere 9
Australia 50, 51
Austria 34, 37
Avarua 55
axis of Earth 8
Ayers Rock see Uluru
Azerbaijan 42, 43

B

Baghdad 42
Bahamas 14, 15
Bahrain 42, 44
Bairiki 50
Balkans 38
Baltic states 35
Bamako 26
Bandar Seri Begawan 47
Bangkok 47
Bangladesh 42, 45
Bangui 26
Banjul 26
Beijing 47
Beirut 42
Belarus 38, 39

Belgium 34, 36
Belgrade 34
Belize 13, 15
Belmopan 15
Benelux countries 36
Benin 26, 28
Berlin 34
Bern 34
Bhutan 42, 45
biomes 32
Bishkek 42
Bissau 26
Black Sea 37, 39
Bloemfontein 31
Bogotá 18
Boku 42
Bolivia 18, 20, 21
Bosnia & Herzegovina 34, 38
Botswana 30, 31
Brasilia 18, 19
Bratislava 34
Brazil 18, 19
Brazzaville 31
Brunei 46, 47
Brussels 34, 36
Bucharest 39
Budapest 34, 37
Buenos Aires 23
Bujumbura 31
Bulgaria 37, 39
Burkina Faso 26, 27
Burma 46, 47
Burundi 30, 31

C

Cairo 26
California 12
Cambodia 46, 47
Cameroon 29, 31
Canada 11, 15
Canberra 50, 51
Cape Horn 23
Cape Town 31
Cape Verde 26, 28
Caracas 18, 22
Caribbean 15
Caucasus 43
Cayenne 18
Central Africa 29
Central African Republic 26, 29
Central Asia 44
Central Europe 37
Central Southern Africa 30
Central Southern Asia 45
Chad 26, 29
Chile 20, 23
China 45, 47, 48
Chisinau 39
Christian nations 29, 37, 43
cliffs 25

climate 32–33
clouds 33
coastal erosion 25
Colombia 18, 22
Colombo 42
Comoros 30, 31
Conakry 26
Congo 29, 31
Congo River/Basin and Valley 29, 31
continents, land area 58
Cook Islands 53, 54, 55
Copenhagen 34
Costa Rica 13, 15
Croatia 34, 38
Cuba 14, 15
Cyprus 37, 42
Czech Republic 34, 37

DEF

Dakar 26
Damascus 42
Danube River 39
Dead Sea 42, 44
Democratic Republic of Congo 29, 31
Denmark 34, 35
deserts 24
Dhaka 42
Dili 47
Djibouti 26, 29
Dodoma 31
Doha 42
Dominican Republic 14, 15
Dublin 34
Dushanbe 42
Earth 8–9, 16–17, 58
earthquakes 17
East Africa 29
East Asia 45
East Timor 46, 47
Easter Island 53, 54, 55
eclipses 9
Ecuador 18, 21
Egypt 26, 27
El Salvador 13, 15
England 35
Equator 8, 40
Equatorial Guinea 29, 31
Eritrea 26, 29
erosion 24–25
Estonia 35, 39
Ethiopia 26, 29
Europe 34–39, 48, 58
European Union (EU) 35, 36
Fiji 53, 55
Finland 34, 35, 39
Fongafale 55
France 34, 36
Fray Bentos 19
Freetown 26
French Guiana 18, 22

French Polynesia 53, 54, 55

GH

Gabarone 31
Gabon 29, 31
Gambia 26, 28
Gaza Strip 42, 44
Georgetown 18
Georgia 42, 43
Germany 34, 36
Ghana 26, 28
glaciers 24
Gobi Desert 47
Gold Coast 28
Great Barrier Reef 50, 52, 55
Great Lakes 10, 15
Great Plains 10
Great Rift Valley 31
Greater Antilles 15
Greece 37, 39
greenhouse effect 32
Greenland 10, 11
Guam 50, 53
Guatemala 13, 15
Guatemala City 15
Guianas 22
Guinea 26, 28
Guinea Bissau 26, 28
Guinea Coast 28
Gulf of Mexico 12, 15
Gulf States 44
Guyana 18, 22
Hagatna 50
Haiti 14, 15
Hanoi 47
Harare 31
Havana 15
Hawaiian Islands 53, 55
heat erosion 24
Helsinki 39
Himalayas 17, 42, 47
Hispaniola 14
Honduras 13, 15
Honiara 50
Horn of Africa 26, 29
hot spots 41
Hungary 34, 37
hurricanes 12, 13, 15, 32

IJKL

Iberian Peninsula 36
ice erosion 24
Iceland 34, 35
India 42
Indian Ocean 30
Indian subcontinent 45
Indonesia 46, 47
International Date Line 55
Iran 42, 44
Iraq 42, 44
Ireland 34, 35

Islamabad 42
Israel 42, 44
Italy 34, 37
Ivory Coast 26, 28
Jakarta 47, 49
Jamaica 14, 15
Japan 46, 47
Jordan 42, 44
Jupiter 9
Kabul 42
Kalahari Desert 31
Kampala 31
Kathmandu 42
Kazakhstan 42, 44, 45
Kenya 29, 31
Khartoum 26, 27
Kiev 38, 39
Kigali 31
Kingston 15
Kinshasa 31
Kiribati 50, 53
Kuala Lumpur 47
Kuwait 42, 44
Kyrgyzstan 42, 44, 45
La Paz 18, 20
Laayoune 26
Lake Bailal 47
Lake Chad 29
Lake Nicaragua 13
Lake Titicaca 18, 21
lakes, largest 58
languages 49
Laos 47
latitude 8
Latvia 35, 39
Lebanon 42, 43
Leeward Islands 14
Lesotho 30, 31
Lesser Antilles 15
Liberia 26, 28
Libreville 31
Libya 26, 27
lightning 32
Lilongwe 31
Lima 18
Lisbon 34
Lithuania 35, 39
Lomé 26
London 34
longitude 8
Low Countries 36
Luanda 31
Lubljana 34
Lusaka 31
Luxembourg 34, 36

M

Gage, Phineas 54
Macedonia 34, 38
Madagascar 30, 31
Madrid 34
Maghreb 26, 27
magnetic poles 16
Majuro Atoll 50

Malabo 31
Malawi 30, 31
Malaysia 46, 47
Maldives 42, 45
Mali 26, 27
Malta 34, 37
Managua 15
Manama 42
Manila 47
Maputo 31
Mariana Trench 55
Mars 8
Marshall Islands 50, 53
Maseru 31
Mata'Utu 55
Mauritania 26, 27
Mauritius 30, 31
Mbabane 31
Mediterranean Sea 34, 37, 39
Melanesia 51, 53
Melekeok 50
Mercury 8
Mexico 13, 15
Mexico City 13, 15, 49
Micronesia 50, 51, 53
Midway Islands 55
Minsk 39
Mississippi–Missouri 12, 15, 58
Mogadishu 31
Moldova 38, 39
Monaco 34, 36
Mongolia 45, 46, 47
Monrovia 26
Montenegro 34, 38
Montevideo 23
Montserrat 14
Moon 9, 40
Morocco 26, 27
Moroni 31
Moscow 38, 39
Mount Aconcagua 23, 58
Mount Everest 47, 58
mountains, highest by continent 58
Mozambique 30, 31
Muscat 42
Myanmar see Burma

NO

Nairobi 31
Namibia 30, 31
Nassau 15
Nauru 50, 53
Ndjamena 26
Near East 43
Nepal 42, 45
Neptune 8
Netherlands 34, 36
New Caledonia 50
New Delhi 42, 49
New Guinea 52
New York 12, 49

New Zealand 50, 54
Niagara Falls 10, 11
Niamey 26
Nicaragua 13, 15
Nicosia 42
Niger 26, 27
Niger Valley 27
Nigeria 26, 28
Nile River/Valley 26, 27, 58
Niue 53, 54, 55
North America 10–15, 48, 58
North European Plain 39
North Korea 46, 47
North Pole 8, 56
North Sea 34
Northern Ireland 35
Northern Mariana Islands 50, 53
Norway 34, 35
Nouakchott 26
Nouméa 50
Nuku'Alofa 55
Nuuk 10
Oceania 48, 50–55, 58
oceans 40–41
Okavanga Delta 31
Oman 42, 44
Oslo 34
Ottawa 15
Ouagadougou 26
Outback 50, 52

PQR
Pacific Ocean 40, 55
Pago Pago 55
Pakistan 42, 45
Palau 50, 53
Palestine 44
Palikir 50
Pampas 20, 23

Panama 14, 15
Panama Canal 14
Panama City 15
Papeete 55
Papua New Guinea 50, 52
Paraguay 20, 23
Paramaribo 18, 22
Paris 34
Patagonia 20
Persian Gulf 42
Peru 18, 21
Philippines 46, 47
Phnom Penh 47
Pitcairn Islands 53, 54, 55
planets 8, 9
plates see tectonic plates
Podgorica 34
Poland 34, 36
polar regions 56–57
political systems 49
Polynesia 51, 53
population 48–49
Port Louis 31
Port Moresby 50
Port-Au-Prince 15
Port-of-Spain 15
Porto-novo 26
Portugal 34, 36
Port-Vila 50
Prague 34, 37
Praia 26
Prairies 11
Pretoria 31
Puerto Rico 14, 15
Punta Arenas 20
Pyong Yang 47
Qatar 42, 44
Québec 11
Quito 18
Rabat 26
rain forest 18, 19, 29, 31

Rangoon 47
Red Sea 26, 42
religions 14, 15, 36, 37, 49
Reykjavik 34
Riga 39
rivers 25, 58
Riyadh 42
Rocky Mountains (Rockies) 10, 11, 15
rocks 17
Romania 38, 39
Rome 34, 37
Rotterdam 36
Russian Federation 38, 39, 43, 47, 48
Rwanda 30, 31

S
Sahara 26
Sahel 26
St. Martin 14
St. Petersburg 38
Saipan 50
Samoa 53, 55
San José 15
San Juan 15
San Marino 34, 37
San Salvador 15
Sana 42
Santiago 23
Santo Domingo 15
São Paulo 19, 49
São Tomé 31
Sao Tome & Principe 29, 31
Sarajevo 34
Saturn 8
Saudi Arabia 42, 44
Scandinavia 34, 35
Scotland 35
seafloor spreading 40

seasons 8
Senegal 26, 28
Seoul 47, 49
Serbia 34, 38
Seychelles 30, 31
Siberia 43, 47
Sierra Leone 26, 28
Singapore 46, 47
Skopje 34, 38
Slovakia 34, 37
Slovenia 34, 37
Sofia 39
Solar System 8
Solomon Islands 50, 53
Somalia 29, 31
South Africa 30, 31
South America 18–23, 48, 58
South Korea 46, 47
South Pole 8, 57
southeast Asia 46
Southern Africa 30
Spain 34, 36
Sri Lanka 42, 45
steppes 47
Stockholm 34
storms 32
Sucre 18, 20
Sudan 26, 27
Suez Canal 27
Sun 8, 9, 32, 40
Suriname 18, 22
Suva 55
Swaziland 30, 31
Sweden 34, 35
Switzerland 34, 37
Syria 42, 43

TUV
Taipei 47
Taiwan 46, 47
Tajikstan 42, 44, 45

Tallinn 35, 39
Tanzania 30, 31
Tashkent 42
Tbilisi 42
tectonic plates 16, 17, 40, 41
Tegucigalpa 15
Tehran 42
Tel Aviv 42
Thailand 46, 47
The Hague 34
Thimpu 42
thunder 32
tides 40
Tirana 34
Togo 26, 28
Tokelau 53, 54, 55
Tokyo 47, 49
Tonga 53, 55
tornadoes 12, 33
Trinidad & Tobago 15
Tripoli 26
Tshwane 31
Tunis 26
Tunisia 26, 27
Turkey 39, 42, 43
Turkmenistan 42, 44, 45
Tuvalu 53, 55
UAE 42, 44
Uganda 30, 31
UK 34, 35
Ukraine 38, 39
Ulan Bator 47
Uluru (Ayers Rock) 50, 51
United States 12, 15
Uranus 8
Uruguay 19, 23
Uzbekistan 42, 44, 45
Valletta 34
Vanuatu 50, 53
Vatican City 34, 37, 48
vegetation zones 32

Venezuela 18, 22
Venus 8
Victoria 31
Vienna 34
Vientiane 47
Vietnam 46, 47
Vilnius 39
volcanoes 13, 17, 20, 41

WXYZ
Wales 35
Wallis and Futuna 53, 55
Warsaw 34
Washington, D.C. 12, 15
water cycle 33
water erosion 25
waterfalls 18, 30, 58
wealth 49
weather 32–33
Wellington 50
West Bank 42
Western Sahara 26
Windhoek 31
winds 24, 32, 33, 40
Windward Islands 14
Yamoussoukro 26, 28
Yaoundé 31
Yemen 42, 44
Yellowstone 12
Yerevan 42
Zagreb 34
Zambia 30, 31
Zimbabwe 30, 31

Acknowledgments

The publisher would like to thank Lynn Bresler for proofreading and the index.

My work here is done... Welcome to Snowdomia!

what a view!

ARCTIC OCEAN

NORTH AMERICA

EUROPE

ATLANTIC OCEAN

AFRICA

SOUTH AMERICA

PACIFIC OCEAN

ANTARCTICA